PRAISE FOR
EVERY ROSE HAS ITS THORN

"It's perfect for figuring out what type of guy you are, and more important, what type of guy the jerk who's dating your ex-girlfriend is."
—Frank Lesser, writer, *The Colbert Report*

"Finally, somebody has assembled the definitive field guide to guys, targeted to awesome chicks who can all do better."
—Julie Klausner, author of *I Don't Care About Your Band*

"It's frightening how accurately Erin Bradley has identified the modern rock-dude archetypes. *Every Rose Has Its Thorn* is a must-own for music fans who want clever books in their bathrööms."
—Scott Lapatine, founder, Stereogum.com

"This book is all you need to find the right guy, because you don't really know who you slept with until you roll over and sneak a look at their iPod."
—Mike Albo, author of *Hornito* and *The Underminer: The Best Friend Who Casually Destroys Your Life*

"*Every Rose Has Its Thorn* made me want to get a sex-change operation, because I can't imagine anything more fun than being a woman and getting together with my girlfriends and reading aloud from it while drinking huge glasses of wine and high-fiving each other."
—David Rees, author of *My New Fighting Technique Is Unstoppable* and *Get Your War On*

"I found this book very demeaning to men and most specifically to men who rock."
—Phil Costello, mastermind behind the greatest tribute band of all time, Tragedy: All-Metal Tribute to the Bee Gees

"Erin is a supersmart, superfunny writer, and this is a supersmart, superfunny book. Like a relationship, it will make you feel like either a douchebag or a rock star. Maybe both."
—DC Pierson, author of *The Boy Who Couldn't Sleep and Never Had To*

"*Every Rose Has Its Thorn* is a hilarious playlist ripped and burned directly from Erin Bradley's love life. Reading it is like having her stand outside your window blasting wisdom from a boombox."

—Rob Kutner, writer, *The Tonight Show with Conan O'Brien* and *The Daily Show*,
and author of *Apocalypse How: Turn the End Times into the Best of Times!*

"*Every Rose Has Its Thorn* is a hilarious, fun, and useful dating guide for cool women. It's also a super-entertaining trip down memory lane—most women will find more than one past paramour lurking in these pages. Various types of men will see themselves represented here too, either to their delight or to their chagrin. Highly recommended for rock'n'roll-loving ladies, both single and attached."

—Laura Barcella, writer for *The Village Voice*, Salon, and *Time Out New York*

"With unnerving accuracy, the Bradley sisters dissect the inner emotional workings of modern urban manhood in all its variations. Underlying it all is the refreshing insight that men are just people too. Horribly imperfect people. None of whom have any idea what it is like to date them."

—Steve Huey, writer, *Yacht Rock* and AllMusicGuide.com

"Erin Bradley offers a hilarious take on the guys you'll meet at your local dive bar or rock club, with warnings on whom to avoid and whom to saunter backstage after and seduce. *Every Rose* is a witty take on our favorite sexy rock stars and should be required reading before you toss your bra onstage or quit your job to follow his tour bus." —Rachel Kramer Bussel, editor of *Fast Girls: Erotica for Women*

"Whether you've had a bad boyfriend, you've been a bad boyfriend, or you've had to stand by and watch as your best girlfriend slowly drifted into a relationship train wreck, you'll find yourself alternately laughing and nodding your head as you make your way through *Every Rose Has Its Thorn*. Erin Bradley's book is the best kind of funny, the smart kind of funny that also rings true. After you read this yourself, you're going to want to buy a copy for each of your girlfriends, with certain entries bookmarked."

—Liam McEneaney, comedian and writer, Comedy Central's *Premium Blend* and VH1's *Best Week Ever*

EVERY ROSE HAS ITS THORN

ERIN BRADLEY

Illustrations by Heather Bradley

JEREMY P. TARCHER/PENGUIN

a member of Penguin Group (USA) Inc.

New York

EVERY ROSE HAS ITS THORN

The Rock 'n' Roll Field Guide to Guys

JEREMY P. TARCHER/PENGUIN
Published by the Penguin Group
Penguin Group (USA) Inc., 375 Hudson Street, New York, New York 10014, USA • Penguin Group (Canada), 90 Eglinton Avenue East, Suite 700, Toronto, Ontario M4P 2Y3, Canada (a division of Pearson Penguin Canada Inc.) • Penguin Books Ltd, 80 Strand, London WC2R 0RL, England • Penguin Ireland, 25 St Stephen's Green, Dublin 2, Ireland (a division of Penguin Books Ltd) • Penguin Group (Australia), 250 Camberwell Road, Camberwell, Victoria 3124, Australia (a division of Pearson Australia Group Pty Ltd) • Penguin Books India Pvt Ltd, 11 Community Centre, Panchsheel Park, New Delhi–110 017, India • Penguin Group (NZ), 67 Apollo Drive, Rosedale, North Shore 0632, New Zealand (a division of Pearson New Zealand Ltd) • Penguin Books (South Africa) (Pty) Ltd, 24 Sturdee Avenue, Rosebank, Johannesburg 2196, South Africa

Penguin Books Ltd, Registered Offices: 80 Strand, London WC2R 0RL, England

Copyright © 2010 by Erin Bradley
Illustrations copyright © 2010 by Heather Bradley
All rights reserved. No part of this book may be reproduced, scanned, or distributed in any printed or electronic form without permission. Please do not participate in or encourage piracy of copyrighted materials in violation of the author's rights. Purchase only authorized editions. Published simultaneously in Canada

Most Tarcher/Penguin books are available at special quantity discounts for bulk purchase for sales promotions, premiums, fund-raising, and educational needs. Special books or book excerpts also can be created to fit specific needs. For details, write Penguin Group (USA) Inc. Special Markets, 375 Hudson Street, New York, NY 10014.

Library of Congress Cataloging-in-Publication Data

Bradley, Erin.
   Every rose has its thorn : the rock 'n' roll field guide to guys / Erin Bradley ; illustrations by Heather Bradley.
     p.   cm.
   ISBN 978-1-58542-774-1
   1. Man–woman relationships.   2. Single women.   3. Mate selection.   4. Rock musicians.   I. Title.
   HQ801.B845   2010   2010002138
   158.2—dc22

Printed in the United States of America
10 9 8 7 6 5 4 3 2 1

BOOK DESIGN BY MEIGHAN CAVANAUGH

Neither the publisher nor the author is engaged in rendering professional advice or services to the individual reader. The ideas, procedures, and suggestions contained in this book are not intended as a substitute for consulting with a physician. All matters regarding your health require medical supervision. Neither the author nor the publisher shall be liable or responsible for any loss or damage allegedly arising from any information or suggestion in this book.

While the author has made every effort to provide accurate telephone numbers and Internet addresses at the time of publication, neither the publisher nor the author assumes any responsibility for errors, or for changes that occur after publication. Further, the publisher does not have any control over and does not assume any responsibility for author or third-party websites or their content.

WE'D LIKE TO DEDICATE THIS BOOK TO MOM AND DAD,

THE COOLEST PARENTS ANY SISTERS COULD EVER HAVE,

AND OUR OWN PERSONAL ROCK STARS.

CONTENTS

OPENING ACT — 1

1. BAD COMPANY — 4
2. JOHNNY B. GOODE — 34
3. SEXY MOTHERFUCKER — 66
4. MANNISH BOY — 96
5. PART-TIME LOVER — 126

6. MR. BIG STUFF — 138

7. THE BOY WITH THE THORN IN HIS SIDE — 170

8. SWEET CHILD O' MINE — 204

9. FATHER FIGURE — 236

10. MR. ROBOTO — 270

AFTER PARTY — 301

EVERY ROSE HAS ITS THORN

EAST VILLAGE, NYC 03:17 AM FRIDAY

heather   Erin

OPENING ACT

It was Clint Eastwood playing Dirty Harry or perhaps a cynical online dater who once said, "Bands are like assholes. Everyone's got one."

Whether you're dating a real-life rock star or someone who guzzles Rockstar energy drink to get that extra boost he needs to get through another two hours of *Law & Order*, chances are you'll find him in one of these ten chapters.

But hold on to your limited-edition Bon Jovi poster, because you'll find a whole lot more. Information such as:

- Where to meet him
- Recommended pickup tactics
- What he's like as a boyfriend
- What he's like as booty call
- Exit strategies for when it's over

For those of you not into the whole reading thing, there are also plenty of illustrations, including celebrity likenesses just begging for a doodled-on mustache or a set of Viking horns.

Did we mention the musical playlists and quizzes? What about the helpful infographics and true-life anecdotes from women who've been there, done that, bought the T-shirt, then lost it when they made a quick getaway after sleeping over?

Show-off stuff aside, this book is about fun. It is not meant to disparage men, musicians, the Canadian harp seal, or anyone bearing more than a passing resemblance to Kenny Loggins.

You'll find some stereotyping in these pages, none of which should be taken any more seriously than that "Men Are from Mars, Women Are Shoe-Obsessed Nurturers Who Hate Sex and Maintain Romantic Relationships with Their Household Cleaning Equipment" rigmarole. We love men almost as much as we love a Mötley Crüe drum solo. Our hope is that by sharing our experiences, we can get you laughing (or cringing, more likely) about yours.

Now, grab your reading glasses and put on your best pair of leopard-print spandex. We're about to go on a little tour. . . .

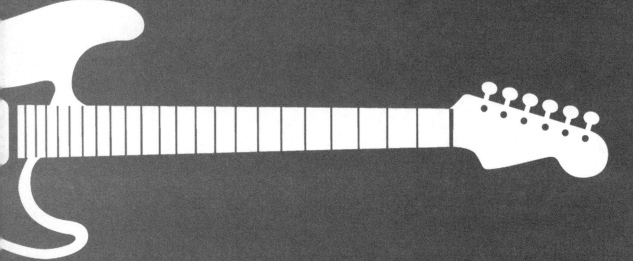

PANY

Fig. 1a: Bad Company

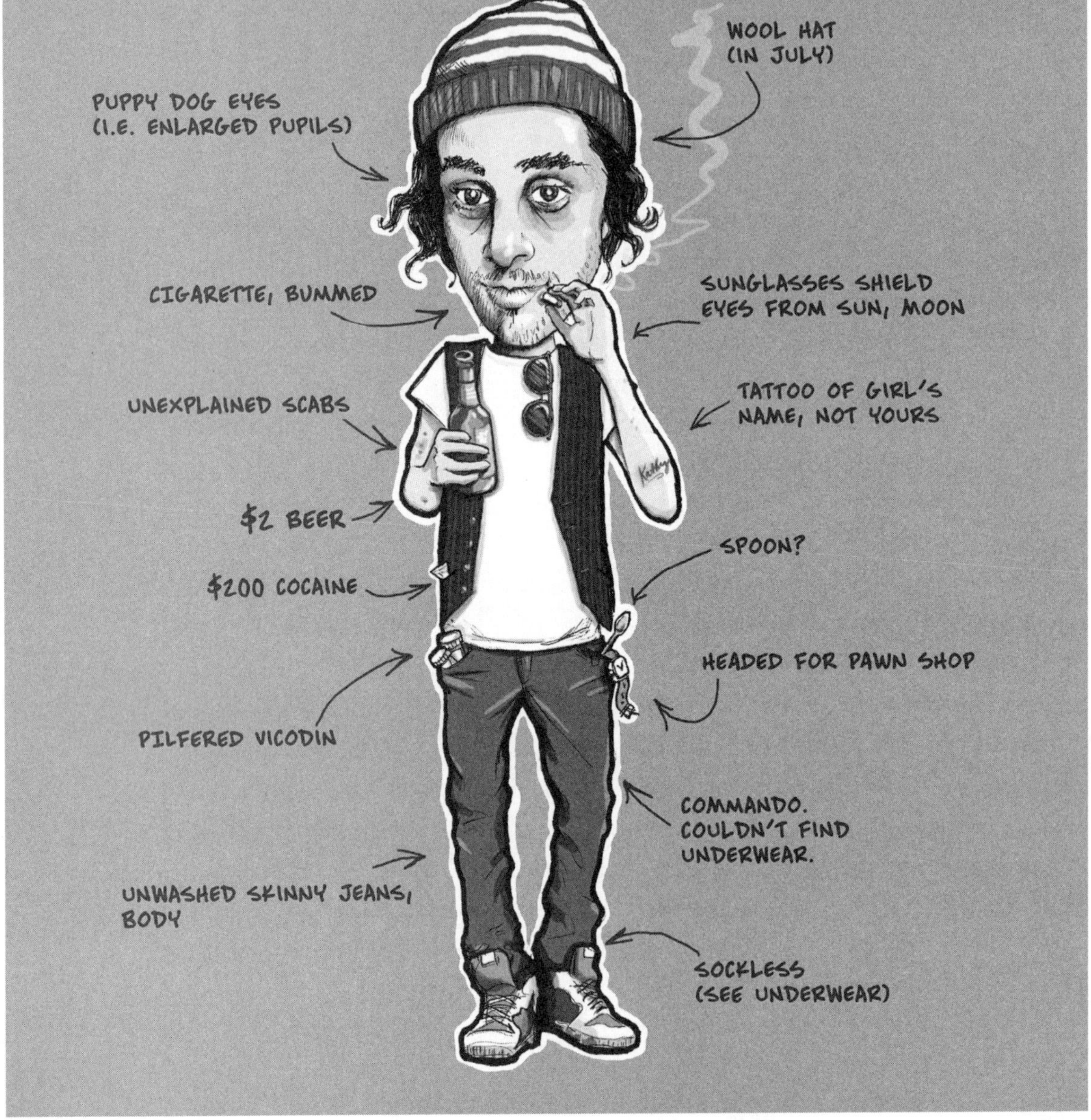

- WOOL HAT (IN JULY)
- PUPPY DOG EYES (I.E. ENLARGED PUPILS)
- CIGARETTE, BUMMED
- SUNGLASSES SHIELD EYES FROM SUN, MOON
- UNEXPLAINED SCABS
- TATTOO OF GIRL'S NAME, NOT YOURS
- $2 BEER
- $200 COCAINE
- SPOON?
- HEADED FOR PAWN SHOP
- PILFERED VICODIN
- COMMANDO. COULDN'T FIND UNDERWEAR.
- UNWASHED SKINNY JEANS, BODY
- SOCKLESS (SEE UNDERWEAR)

THE MEET & GREET

Who He Is

An unstable mess in irresistible packaging—the reason Life Skills courses should be mandatory at all public schools and colleges. A boozer. A user. A regular patron of emergency rooms, check-cashing places, and Hallmark Gold Crown stores. All of the crazy of dating a real-life rock star without the fame, fortune, or cushy tour bus.

What He's All About

Avoiding reality, seeking out confrontation, and finding that sweet spot between hedonism and survival. Bad Company is the king of playing off the sympathies of others. If it weren't for his carefully maintained network of enablers, he'd most likely be homeless or, even worse, working steady employment. He makes bad decision after bad decision, yet operates under the assumption that the world is out to get him rather than accepting ownership of his problems. On the plus side, he's ridiculously attractive. Other adjectives include intuitive, charming, and loyal. He may flunk at life, but when it comes to having fun, he's in advanced placement. Bad Company is the guy you warned yourself about. Your head says no, your heart says, "Fuck it, why not?"

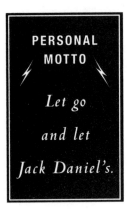

> **PERSONAL MOTTO**
>
> *Let go and let Jack Daniel's.*

Turn-ons

Bottle returns, free food, roll-your-own cigarettes, faux suicide threats, breaking up, getting back together, "borrowing" your ATM card, scratch-offs, pay-as-you-go cell phones.

Turnoffs

Your day job, your best friend, your roommate, your dad, your mom, fruits and vegetables, anything that requires being at a certain place at a certain time, AA meetings, formal wear, suggestions to "cut down."

THE HEADLINERS

All musicians misbehave. It's practically part of the record contract. Standing out requires a certain brand of *je ne sais fuck it*—that blend of pretty boy meets human wreckage otherwise known as Bad Company.

Let's start with an Oliver Twist indie type who's always "Please sir, may I have another?" when it comes to leggy models and heroin, continue with a folk icon who parties like . . . well . . . someone who's not a folk icon, and finish with a Grammy winner high on wine, women, and cough syrup.

Every Rose Has Its Thorn

PETE DOHERTY

Who He Is
English singer/songwriter, founder of the Libertines, Babyshambles front man when he remembers, astrologically a Pisces, which makes him "mysterious," "altruistic," "passionate," and "prone to lesions."

"I'm vain because I'm imperfect."

Pete Doherty,
The Sunday Times,
May 14, 2006

What Makes Him Such Bad Company
Unable to learn from prior mistakes, keeps getting arrested for the same things, keeps making and breaking the same promises, keeps doing the same drugs. It's like that movie *Groundhog Day*, set in a urine-soaked gutter in East London.

Bad Company Highlights
- Day-to-day life so out of control that he was dumped by supermodel-cum-healthy-living-advocate Kate Moss.
- Used to work as a gravedigger, now just looks like walking corpse.
- Got chewed out by Oasis singer and fellow mess Liam Gallagher for doing a crap job of being a father. Way to set the bar.

JAMES TAYLOR

"I probably was not a very good companion."

James Taylor on his marriage to Carly Simon, CBS interview with Charlie Rose, August 21, 2002

Who He Is
Grammy-winning singer, songwriter, and guitarist; one of the few heroin addicts your mom ever had the hots for; Carly Simon's ex-husband; the guy who sings "Fire and Rain" and all those other songs you hear when the utility company puts you on hold.

What Makes Him Such Bad Company
Made music and/or shared drug paraphernalia with just about every other musician of his generation, from Garfunkel to Harrison to Crosby to the Beach Boys to Joni Mitchell; was greasy-faced, long-haired, and strung out long before it was cool to be; got sober and debuted his twenty-fourth album on *Oprah*.

Bad Company Highlights
+ If photos are any indication, didn't crack a smile until he reached the age of forty. All you angsty fourteen-year-olds with guitars, Google-image-search him if you want to see "brooding and surly" done right.
+ Spent time in and out of various mental institutions; during the draft was actually taken away by the proverbial men in little white coats.
+ Charmed everyone with his sweet, confessional melodies, including "Shower the People," a song about showing affection for the ones you love. Carly Simon would divorce him later, saying he didn't spend enough time with her and their children.

Every Rose Has Its Thorn

SOMEWHERE PEOPLE ARE SHIT-FACED OR THE EXACT OPPOSITE

Bad Company isn't the best at handling his substances. He's either getting drunk ("making it an early night"), completely obliterated ("having a couple drinks with friends"), or winding up in a facility with the word *new* or *hope* or *beginnings* on the sign out front ("tying one on"). When that gets old or the court orders it, Bad Company will be at NA or AA meetings, trying to bring his demons under control. Note we said "control," not "quit." Bad Company is still under the impression that he can do a little bit of substance abuse, which we all know is a total joke, like when you divide your entrée in half and ask for a carryout box. He's no more able to stop after one drink than you are not to eat the rest of that bacon ranch shrimp Alfredo. Quitting this guy won't be easy, whether you meet on church basement folding chairs or bar stools.

His Act

aka Ways of Working the Crowd . . .

GIVING OFF DISTRESS SIGNALS

Behind Bad Company's immature, ego-fueled swagger is an even more infantile and arrogant little boy, screaming for help. It takes a special kind of woman to hit on the one man at the Kentwood Association Spring Gala with an outstanding warrant, but there are those who will. It's a whistle heard by only the most vulnerable of women—an almost supernatural experience, what nuns refer to as "The Calling."

GIVING OFF SEX SIGNALS

Bad Company may be terrible at critical thinking and self-control, but sex appeal is an area where he's a natural. He has a few patented moves that he's been using since grade school, such as "Let's turn out the lights and see what happens!" and "I'll show you mine, even if you refuse to show me yours." There's also the never-fail, the old standby—"The Look." Wherever you are, whatever you do, he's staring. You know what that look means. It's the same look Ken gives Barbie right before they mash plastic torsos.

GIVING OFF ODORS

Now, please don't read the above and assume we're talking exclusively dirty and foul. Yes, Bad Company usually smells like BO, metabolized whiskey, and perhaps a hint of overcrowded dollar store. Yet it's kind of a turn-on. Which scent evokes more memories? The sterilized air of a Bed Bath & Beyond or the dank musk of a dive bar? When Bad Company does elect to shower, the resulting scent is even more enticing—dollar-store shampoo and squeaky-clean industrial-strength soap, the kind your father used to use—Irish Spring, Lava, or Dial. It's a heady mixture of nostalgia and pheromones. Unfortunately, Calvin Klein has yet to perfect a facsimile for either. In the meantime, get an old T-shirt, dump half a can of flat beer and the contents of a partially full ashtray on it, soak it in Febreze, and give it to your dog. Once he's napped on it a little while, you should be good to go.

His Wardrobe

aka Proper & Improper Attire . . .

Fig. 1b:
The Drink Getter—
from kitsch to cocktails
in two seconds flat.

LEATHER, LACE, AND A GREASY FACE

Accidental. Is that a philosophy? Bad Company always looks good, even when he looks like hell. He's the kind of dude who can roll out of bed, put on something he found crumpled up next to the nightstand, and still manage to look dashing, if not a little shopworn.

What He Wears

- **Band T-shirts:** Usually slipped to him for free from the girl at the merch table who thought his Scottish accent was sexy. (He wasn't Scottish, just drunk.)
- **Jeans:** Filthy dirty, often designer. A rich socialite ex bought them with the proceeds from her trust fund.
- **Drink-getters:** A pair of alligator-skin boots, a vintage T-shirt that says "My other T-shirt is a Porsche," a taxidermy belt buckle. Bad Company knows that wasted people *love* buying free cocktails for the guy with the amusing accessory. It's like a push-up bra, but for alcoholics.
- **Hats:** All varieties: wool knit, baseball, cowboy, fedora. If it covers his scalp, it's all gravy. In fact, that's also the consistency of his greasy hairdo.

Bad Company

- **Mysterious markings:** Bruises. Tattoos. Words written in Sharpie. Bits of glitter. He's like Pigpen in the *Peanuts* comic strip, only instead of repelling all the little girls, his filth just makes them want to jock him more.

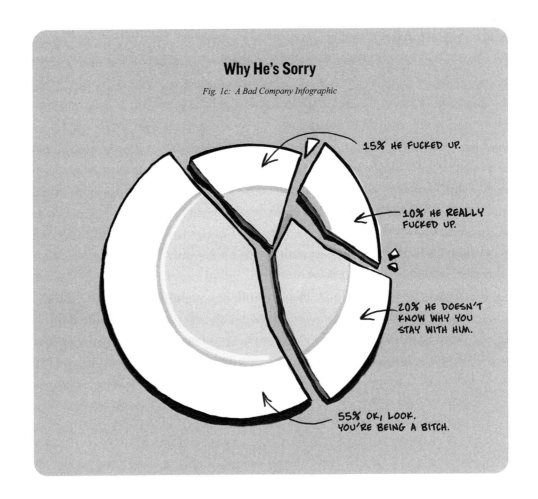

Why He's Sorry

Fig. 1c: A Bad Company Infographic

- 15% HE FUCKED UP.
- 10% HE REALLY FUCKED UP.
- 20% HE DOESN'T KNOW WHY YOU STAY WITH HIM.
- 55% OK, LOOK. YOU'RE BEING A BITCH.

How to Get Backstage

or at the Very Least His
Phone Number . . .

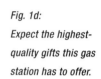

Fig. 1d: Expect the highest-quality gifts this gas station has to offer.

BE THE NEW GIRL

Bad Company is the hard liquor of men—the one that everyone has tried, had a bad experience with, and sworn off, yet still, every day, new people keep trying. You'd think there'd be some sort of wristband system in place or a formalized protocol for warning others. Just know that if you're new to a scene, a neighborhood, or an employer, it won't be long before Bad Company will seek you out. It's your date with Destiny, minus the door-opening and flowers.

Why It Works

Bad Company finds ingénues attractive because of his tendency to bucket women into the categories of Madonna and Whore. Madonnas are perfect women he's just starting to date who don't know he's a fuckup. Whores are ex-girlfriends who have gently but firmly told him he is no longer allowed to spend his weekdays lolling about the apartment in their roommate's robe. You are the former. Unsullied. Untouched. Good to feel that way, doesn't it? Don't get too excited. Like a whiskey-fueled boner, this won't last for long.

PUT ON YOUR BLINDERS

It takes a special kind of person to look at an abandoned junkyard and see a lush garden, full of roses. Too bad you suck at gardening. Finding a Bad Company means culling down that grand vision of the Ultimate Boyfriend into something more realistic. Overlook the spotty hygiene, the lack of friends, the mood swings—and focus on what he does well. For every Bad Company is wholly brilliant at something—lock picking, crewelwork, memorizing Black Sabbath lyrics. You've heard of the phrase "tortured artist." You think Axl was good at being prompt? You think Keith Richards was a master of self-control? Why must you always be so critical?

Why It Works

Bad Company is good at making his good points the most prominent points about him. If it's a penis, he'll fuck you incessantly. If it's his guitar, he'll play it for you everywhere, even outside your bathroom door while you're doin' the doo. Bad Company doesn't mind being liked for one quality. He's happy to be liked for *any* quality, because in his mind he's given up on girls. (Restraining orders will do that to a person.)

BE AT THE TOP OF YOUR GAME

Yes, we realize this sounds like an ad for a sports beverage. In less jockish terms, this simply means having a period in your life where everything goes exactly as you want it. Your self-esteem is working its shaky little form up and out of your wastebasket, where it usually resides next to a half-read Dr. Phil book and an

Every Rose Has Its Thorn

empty bottle of Klonopin. You're making friends, remembering to bring an umbrella, happening on amazing vintage furniture at garage sales, and you just met a cute guy.

Why It Works

That "cute guy"? Bad Company. He's kind of like America, in the sense that he gets the best of everything (in this case, you) but still thinks it's okay to trash the place and treat other people however he wants. You'll be at a party, and your halo of happiness and success will impel him to wander over, as will the huge joint you and your friends are toking on. Soon you'll throw over those other guys you were dating to focus exclusively on being miserable with Bad Company. Good luck with that. Let us know how it works out.

Bad Company

PLAYLIST

Uneasy Listening: An Emergency Room Soundtrack for Bad Company's Latest Accidental Mishap or Intentional Overdose

1. **"Bad Medicine"—Bon Jovi, 1988, Mercury Records**
   Side effects include nausea, suede, MILF-pox, and appearances on *Oprah*.
2. **"Dr. Feelgood"—Mötley Crüe, 1989, Elektra**
   This song is about a fictional drug dealer. What's even weirder is that Bad Company knows him.
3. **"Bad Case of Loving You (Doctor, Doctor)"—Robert Palmer, 1979, Island**
   Ordinarily deemed "way too pussy," this song was once sung by Bad Company during a blackout at a karaoke bar in Greektown.
4. **"Calling Dr. Love"—Kiss, 1977, Casablanca**
   We're not undressing for Dr. Love until he provides a valid medical license and moves his office from the back of an '84 Toyota Corolla. We've been tricked before.
5. **"Soul Doctor"—Foreigner, 1992, Atlantic**
   Listening to this '90s-era "Still got it!" track is worse punishment than anything that could possibly be doled out by Bad Company. Be warned.

Every Rose Has Its Thorn

POP QUIZ

Sad Company or Rad Company?
Answer These Seven Simple Relationship Questions and Find Out

1. Who made the first move?
   a. We had sex within thirty minutes of meeting, so it's kind of hard to tell.
   b. We went out five times before he made eye contact.

2. Would you characterize him as more spontaneous or thoughtful?
   a. Spontaneous. Sometimes it's a breakup text, other times it's flowers.
   b. Thoughtful. Dude will spend twenty minutes selecting an avocado.

3. He's going to cook you a meal. What's in his grocery cart?
   a. Several bottles of liquor, some lube, a box of Apple Jacks, and two live lobsters.
   b. Pasta noodles, spaghetti sauce, rice pudding, *Reader's Digest*

4. He secretly loves it when you:
   a. Leave him unattended around your prescriptions.
   b. Offer him a cough drop.

5. The last time you got into it over a sketchy incoming call, it wound up being:
   a. His dealer's dealer.
   b. A wrong number.

6. You know something is bothering him when he:
   a. Invites another girl over.
   b. Doesn't bother with ice cubes when he gets out of bed to fetch you water.

(continued)

SCORING

MOSTLY A'S = BAD COMPANY
This is wrong. Just wrong. And you know it. But that's what you like about it. Have fun, but remember that like attracts like and that old saying about what happens when you lie down with dogs. Ovaries aren't meant to wear flea collars.

MOSTLY B'S = SAD COMPANY
Holy Manilow, this guy's boring. Don't get us wrong; he's obviously nice, but nice like Kenneth from *30 Rock*. And no one wants to date that unless you can totally corrupt him. Then it's kinda hot. Why don't you get on that and send us some photos?

IF YOU DECIDE TO BOOK HIM FOR ONE NIGHT ONLY

aka the Ins and Outs of Being Friends with Benefits . . .

The Pros

HE LOOKS THE PART (AND ACTS IT)

Bad Company is as close as you'll get to fucking a real live rock star, even if he's one of those rare males who's never picked up an instrument. Naked usually

Every Rose Has Its Thorn

equates to goofy and vulnerable, but there's something about Bad Company that makes him look even more badass when he's undressed. Is it the ill-advised tattoos? The scars of unknown origin? It sounds exploitative (and it probably is), but there's something that makes eyes look even sexier when they're heavy-lidded and under the influence. Given the right lighting and mood music, it's easy to close your eyes and imagine you're bedding down with the new and improved Jim Morrison.

HE'S THERE WHEN YOU NEED HIM, SCARCE WHEN YOU DON'T

Bad Company's been in his share of bedrooms, hotel rooms, and halfway houses. He knows this isn't a love connection. Elaborate excuses? Superfluous. Delicate hints? Ha! Just say the word, and he'll gather up his cigarettes and any loose change you've got lying around, hit the fridge to take the last Budweiser, and be out the door. He'll see nothing classless about the fact that you're getting ready to meet with what you accidentally refer to in front of him as "a real date," i.e., a teacher, a lawyer, or anyone who doesn't suck at achieving normalcy. He'll even walk you to the bar and have a couple of shots as a warm-up.

HE'S SWITZERLAND, WITH THE EMOTIONS

Bad Company has feelings, and sex does affect him. However, he's very skilled at compartmentalizing, usually with the aid of generous helpings of drugs and/or alcohol. As such, Bad Company won't pull any surprise bedroom punches. There will be no midnight confessions or sweaty accidental "I love you's." Which is good, but can occasionally be sad, depending on where you are with your menstrual cycle and your mood chart.

The Cons

HE SCARES KITTY

No one's perfect 100 percent of the time, 100 percent of his life, and if you are, well—we're using double protection, because superciliousness is communicable. Although Bad Company knows condoms are a mandatory with you, you're not so sure about the rest of the women he hooks up with. Nor are you sure about his ability to, as your high school health class teacher would say, "make me-friendly decisions." Will you spend hours on WebMD every time you feel a below-the-belt twinge or decide it's not worth the risk and move on?

HE'S A DISTRACTION

There are very small, select periods of your life where you will have the opportunity to be in sexual congress with a guy like this, and as such, you're willing to make significant lifestyle adjustments. God knows you won't be fucking a rock-star grandpa when you're in a nursing home. (Then again, Andrew W.K. looks like he'll age pretty well.) Although he's a great, interesting, thrilling fuck, you can't be dropping everything (including dates with normals) every time you get that call. Well, technically you can; no one's stopping you. Just saying it's probably not in line with your long-term goals.

Every Rose Has Its Thorn

HE'S PHONING IT IN

Getting all that sleep. Not working. Having things paid for by other people. Being a fuckup is stressful! If you're looking for an expert in the art of cunnilingus, Bad Company is not your preferred vendor. He's good at most positions, but it's like a rock anthem: The guitar riffs are big and broad and awesome, but there's not a lot of nuance. You may feel a little disappointed (ripped off, even) when the penis solo is over. You'd ask for an encore, but the lead musician is already asleep and snoring beside you.

IF YOU DECIDE TO MAKE HIM THE HOUSE BAND

aka from Groupie to Girlfriend and Beyond . . .

The Pros

ENDORPHINS ARE NOT AN UNDERWATER MAMMAL

Those who stay with Bad Company know that the highs are high and the lows are low, but for some reason you keep going back for more. It's as if the body adjusts itself to forget about the pain. It's the reason why, after enduring nine months of pain, only to be wrenched apart and sewn back up like a leather coin purse at summer camp, many women still opt to have more than one child: You'll keep going back to Bad Company because your brain is awash in biological chemicals (and maybe a few pharmacological ones as well). Adrenaline and such are powerful. Unlike some guys who will bore the fuck out of you, Bad Company always keeps you hopped up on something. The result is, you want more of him. This version of bliss is all you've got.

FREE TO BE YOU AND (SLIGHTLY PSYCHOTIC) ME

Two words: No judgments. Bad Company does not know when you're acting unhinged. He's always dated women who are unhinged, so he doesn't have that model. Do you think a feral child is going to give an accurate and thorough critique of his foster parents' decision-making skills? Go ahead—pop sedatives, show up late, don't vote; litter, flake out, stay in the house for seven days, order hundreds of dollars in burritos, get up at four a.m. and start making a papier-mâché sculpture. Bad Company won't fault you for it. He'll probably think it's cool.

VENUS DE BI-LO

Bad Company would rather put you down than compliment you, but he's surprised that a fox like you is taking him seriously enough to go out with him. He's used to being a fuck toy or a tool to piss off parents and nothing further. He figures you to be something of a saint and therefore puts you up there on a pedestal. Well, technically he can't afford a pedestal. It's an old end table covered with cigarette burns and a couple of phone books. It's a small honor but an important one. You like wearing the princess crown, even if it's missing a couple of faux rhinestones.

 *The Cons*

CAN'T WE EVER . . .

Have anything nice? Be on time? Refrain from fighting for more than four hours? Show up sober? Being in a relationship with Bad Company makes even the most mundane tasks feel impossible. It's two people in a tug-of-war against sanity. Bad Company's anti, you're pro, but he's got the bigger biceps. You'll long for a time when everything happened more or less the way it was supposed to and getting through every minute of the day wasn't such a struggle.

DRAIN-O

Energy. You have none. Bad Company has absorbed every last drop. Though he's heavy with the praise (see that pedestal stuff earlier), you spend a lot of time being criticized and defending yourself. You've never really liked yourself a whole lot in the first place, so having to constantly plead your case gets exhausting. Bad Company compliments only when it's easy or necessary to stop the bleeding from one of his recent fuckups. He substitutes cheap gas-station roses (see Fig. 1d) and the beginnings of songs he wrote for you (but will never finish) in lieu of real contrition.

THE KIND YOU DON'T TAKE HOME TO MOTHER

A dark bar where the rest of your friends are already inebriated is about the only place you want to have him meet anyone you know. It gets impractical after a while. Not wanting your boyfriend to meet Mom and Dad can easily be blamed on strict parents. Not wanting your boyfriend to meet distant acquaintances and neighbors you've never met can only be blamed on yourself and your poor choices.

HOW TO END IT HARMONIOUSLY

WITH A SELF-OUTING

No one talks about Bad Company. Who's ever heard of a smug Facebook status update about dating a hoodlum? *"Guess who left me without a ride so he could go off with a questionable-looking girl in search of coke?" "Sheila is watching Jeff run someone off the side of the road!"* Bad Company relationships thrive in secrecy, so make like a *Tyra* show guest and let it out, girl. Be so TMI even the office gossip is telling you to shut it. Once people know what's going on, they're going to keep asking you *if* it's still going on and *why* it's still going on and *when* you're going to do something about it. You'll eventually give in to peer pressure, only this time it will be for the right reasons.

WITH A SPONSOR

A best friend. A family member. A cat whose glare is particularly scornful. Usually there are already quite a few individuals who strongly disapprove of Bad Company and see through all your attempts to talk him up, so it shouldn't be hard. Tell them you want to stop the insanity and that you need their help. Do whatever it takes to show them you're serious. Etch it into a cut-glass paperweight. Give them access to your e-mail and voicemail accounts. Pay them a per diem for surprise inspections and give them stern instructions to punish any relapses accordingly.

WITH A REVERSE "PAY IT FORWARD"

Don't worry about giving Bad Company advance notice, letting him down gently, or any of that rot. Just get the hell out. You do not owe any explanation to the guy with whom you spend more time arguing than you do talking, who pawned your air conditioner and accused you of cheating, then gave you some strain of genital parasite that even your doctor's never heard of. Please be advised we're talking about Bad Company, not abusive fuckholes. For those, you'd best call someone who knows more than we do, such as Jodie Foster or social services. We don't want to trigger anyone who has access to a trigger. Proceed with caution.

HOW TO KEEP MAKING SWEET MUSIC TOGETHER

DIAL DOWN THE DRAMA

We know how it is, when every bit of verbal discourse leads to a blowup and every trip to get garbage bags has a story arc. But guess what? All that arguing takes *effort*. You could be using that time to pump iron or crochet erotic pot holders. The next time Bad Company picks a fight, don't engage. Just walk away. Ignore him. This may sound like we're telling you to be a good little Boston terrier and roll over, but it's really about taking care of yourself. Would you rather get a good night's sleep or spend the next four hours convincing someone who got arrested for shoplifting bobbleheads that you're "not immature"? You can't change his mind or his dysfunctions. You're with him for a reason, so focus on what *does* work and stop screaming yourself hoarse.

KILL IT WITH THE "COMPARE AND CONTRAST"

Why is it that when you're with someone, suddenly everyone else gets hotter? If you're Bad Company's girlfriend, it's rarely a physical attraction that's causing your eyes to wander. Whether it's the guy at your bagel place or your roommate's disgusting boyfriend—the one that sheds pubes all over the bathroom like some kind of macho dandelion—you start to entertain thoughts: "I bet *he's* got more than one pair of shoes," and "I'm sure *her* boyfriend wouldn't call her from a different state at four in the morning." The problem here is that there's no such thing as a person or a relationship that's free of problems. You've chosen

Every Rose Has Its Thorn

to be with this particular mess. If you're not going to leave it, at least learn to love it.

FIX YOUR OWN SHIT BEFORE ASSISTING OTHERS

Forget about him—how are *you* doing? Are you digging the way your life is going? Tumultuous relationships are a great tool for avoidance. Saturday: "I can't work on my writing because I stayed up all night worrying about Bad Company." Sunday: "Sorry, Jane, can't meet you for a run. I'm waiting for Bad Company to call me back so I can hang up on him." Monday: "I meant to get to the office on time, Mrs. Boss, but Bad Company went on a bender last night, and I wanted to make sure he had soda crackers for when he wakes up." Should you take care of your BF when he's hugging the toilet and deconstructing SpaghettiOs? Of course. We're just saying that the relationship will have a lot more longevity if you make yourself top priority.

FOR THE RECORD

aka Relationship Lessons from the School of Rock . . .

IT PAYS TO BE GOOD TO THE LIFERS

Oh, hi. It's your friends and family. You know, the people who've been in your life a lot longer than your current beau, yet you've been blowing off every phone call, e-mail, and social invitation from so you can either fight or fuck with Bad

Company. Now that you're through the thick of it, you're going to need to do some hardcore making-upping. It might not be wise to go all confessional. If there's one thing they want to hear less than the details of your fighting, it's the heartbreak you're feeling over this loser. See if they need any painting done or offer to comb their snooty Persian.

LOVE AS A CHARACTER BUILDER

You've been up. You've been down. You've been mad, sad, furious, elated, and in the depths of despair. The one destination you haven't been? Yawnsville. Bad Company has problems, but putting you to sleep isn't one of them. Though excruciating to go through, there's something about never-a-dull-moment that keeps the tissues flexible and the nervous system shapely and young. And who doesn't want agile neurons? It's an uncertain world out there, folks. If you can get through this relationship, you can get through any relationship, and it's good to have that under your belt.

SANE IS AS SANE DOES

Bad Company is the most out-there guy you've ever been with: He's unpredictable, confrontational, addicted to everything from drama to diphenhydramine. Yet you let him into your life and granted him entry into your special hoo-ha place. Why? What were you getting out of it? What was the payoff? Did it make you feel tortured? Brave? Like a stoic little soldier? Did you like that people were worried about you? Did you secretly admire his rebellion? Understand the answers to these questions, and you'll get closer to understanding yourself. (Just kidding. That happens only in movies with Meryl Streep as the star.)

 Every Rose Has Its Thorn

★★★ Reviews

What Critics Are Saying About Bad Company

"I don't even know if it's so much the sex with these guys that's so attractive as it is someone coming to you and saying 'I am so fucked up, but I neeeeeeeed you so bad!'"

—CASSANDRA

"I dated a Bad Company who broke up with me from jail. We were engaged. He called me up and said, 'I spent the night in jail. I can't do this anymore.'"

—ANGIE

"You get involved with Bad Company because you think he's so cool and so artistic and so interesting, but, if it's like, if you don't have clean underwear, how smart can you be?"

—CELINE

YOUR MINI PRESS KIT

Bad Company is the guy who . . .

✦ May or may not show up to his own birthday party.

✦ Considers a car, a job, and a place to live "nice to have" but mostly optional.

✦ Has a life story that reads like a reverse Horatio Alger novel.

✦ Is self-proclaimed "lazy" about: brushing his teeth, returning monies borrowed, dressing open wounds.

✦ Blurs the line between girlfriend and caseworker.

B. GOODE

2

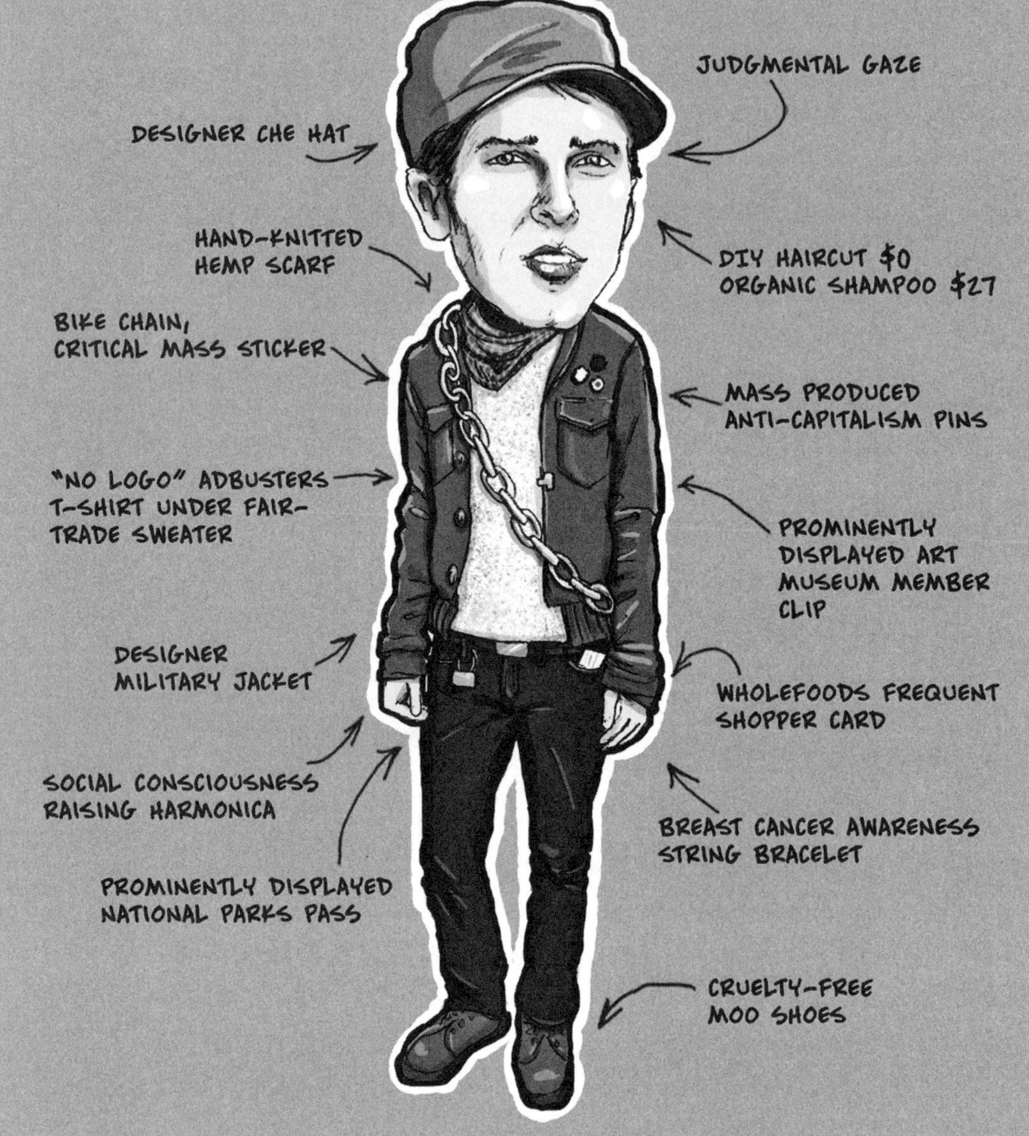

Fig. 2a: Johnny B. Goode

- DESIGNER CHE HAT
- JUDGMENTAL GAZE
- HAND-KNITTED HEMP SCARF
- DIY HAIRCUT $0 ORGANIC SHAMPOO $27
- BIKE CHAIN, CRITICAL MASS STICKER
- MASS PRODUCED ANTI-CAPITALISM PINS
- "NO LOGO" ADBUSTERS T-SHIRT UNDER FAIR-TRADE SWEATER
- PROMINENTLY DISPLAYED ART MUSEUM MEMBER CLIP
- DESIGNER MILITARY JACKET
- WHOLEFOODS FREQUENT SHOPPER CARD
- SOCIAL CONSCIOUSNESS RAISING HARMONICA
- BREAST CANCER AWARENESS STRING BRACELET
- PROMINENTLY DISPLAYED NATIONAL PARKS PASS
- CRUELTY-FREE MOO SHOES

THE MEET & GREET

Who He Is

A letter writer, a volunteer, a believer in mass transit. Johnny B. Goode doesn't own a TV and doesn't want one. He constantly looks for opportunities to display his proud ignorance of pop culture. The kind of person you thought you'd marry when you were young and idealistic and didn't realize how much extra it costs for soy milk. Bono-at-his-most-annoying-meets-boyfriend.

What He's All About

Johnny B. Goode is the king of unsolicited lectures and opinions. It's more important to be right than it is to make human connections. He's the guy who will spend the afternoon working with injured birds of prey and then proceed to get in a vicious fight with your grandpa about politics, despite your prepping him the whole week before not to bring up bisexuality, France, or Barack Obama. As far as good qualities go, Johnny B. Goode is always informed. He believes. He acts. He's doing what he can to make the world suck less. He's not like other guys you date, who make fun of everything or treat it with ironic detachment. He cares about the kind of stuff you care about, and that's why you're so drawn to him.

> **PERSONAL MOTTO**
>
> *Only I can judge you.*

Turn-ons

Fiddles, implied disdain, overseas travel, alternate spellings, vegan cupcakes, adjusting the thermostat to a less comfortable temperature, Cormac McCarthy novels, cardamom.

Turnoffs

"Stock" tattoos, retail businesses, social networking applications, the current decade, copyright protection, displays of public exuberance, rap music less than fifteen years old.

THE HEADLINERS

At first glance, rock 'n' roll rebel and do-gooder seem to be a disconnect. Then you realize rockers are *supposed* to be selfish, destructive, sociopathic pricks. Enter the Johnny B. Goodes, the guys who are willing to do anything—even abstaining from alcohol, fun, or sirloin—to be shocking. *Rebel* is another way of saying *ego*, though neither is the proper spelling of *sanctimonious*.

Here we have a hip-hop legend who's as big into art-house collaborations as he is black T-shirts, a singer-songwriter so into asceticism he married Gwyneth Paltrow, and a hipster with a heart so on fire he wound up going bald.

MOBY

Who He Is
Little. Bald. Different. DJ, musician, blogger, foul-tasting frou-frou iced-tea entrepreneur, collector of clever T-shirts.

What Makes Him Such a Johnny B. Goode
Vegan to the point of making you want to eat stuffed animals in addition to regular animals just to spite him; the only celeb to ever treat taunts from Eminem seriously; uses words like *shan't* and *parlance* in his everyday communication.

"I don't like things very much."

Moby,
Psychology Today,
September 1, 2004

Johnny B. Goode Highlights
- Takes DJing superseriously as an art form. Isn't it just pushing a few buttons and imposing your taste in music on everybody, that music being the sounds of a robot clubbing you in the head with a Speak & Spell?
- Real name is Richard (which, as we all know, is short for you-know-what) but was dubbed Moby by his parents because of a distant family relationship to the big whale book author. You *know* he's been using that story to get laid since he could talk.
- To judge from his relationships, has a completely expected thing for manic pixie dream girls.

His Regular Venues

aka Where You'll Find Him...

AT A NICHE GATHERING

Always on the lookout for the newest version of what's old, Johnny B. Goode hangs with the butchers, the bakers, the soy candlestick makers. He doesn't consciously realize this, but as a former geek he's making up for it by ingratiating himself with the inner-inner-innermost "in crowds." He may or may not participate in the activities, but he wants you to know that he was there and that he supports them—dropping breezy mentions on his Facebook/Flickr/Twitter accounts. Johnny B. Goode is too calculatedly uncalculated to admit it, but he's secretly hoping to run into his female counterpart.

DINING ALFRESCO

While the rest of the sane people are inside, enjoying their artichoke risotto with luxurious comforts like padded chairs, heat, and napkins that don't blow off the tables, Johnny B. Goode is calmly slurping his rainwater/soba noodles on the patio. See how serene his manner? How calm his expression? He looks like a young Parisian, or perhaps Hemingway, scribbling in a Moleskine. He wants you to wonder if he's writing about you. He wants you to want him to be sketching *your* gorgeous visage. You'd go outside to meet him, if only it weren't so damn cozy up at the bar, what with the space heater and complimentary nachos.

AT A HOLIER-THAN-THOU HOLE-IN-THE-WALL

Johnny B. Goode is on a never-ending hunt for the bar with the best backstory, whether it's a Prohibition relic or the premier gay leather bar of the '70s that's been reinvented as a Mecca for organic Japanese sake. Once he's found it, Johnny B. Goode will nearly always be by himself. He'll be drinking the second-best beer on tap, being careful not to order something too highbrow (anything with *dunkel* or *weiss* in the name or a weird-looking monk on the label) or low (Pabst, Schlitz, whatever you can put out a cigarette in, drink, and not notice a significant taste difference). He will not be reading (doesn't want to look like he's trying too hard), nor will he be flirting with the wait staff (he's above it). All of his energies are going into looking like a regular. Which he is, sort of. He's been coming here for over two weeks now.

His Act

aka Ways of Working the Crowd . . .

PASSIVE-AGGRESSIVELY JUDGING

When it comes to cruel and pointed observation, Johnny B. Goode would give the meanest Mean Girl or the bitchiest drag queen a run for her shooties or shanklets or whatever the kids are wearing now. How it's expressed will vary: a snarky text broadcast covertly typed out under the table at dinner; a whisper in the ear of one of his compadres at a show; an aloof posture and bemused stare as fellow party guests engage in a rowdy game of beer pong. A simpleton might ask why Johnny B. Goode doesn't leave if he doesn't like what's going on. Oh, you silly goose. Isn't it obvious? Then he wouldn't be able to feel better than everyone else. Even more important, he won't be able to tell other people about his situational superiority in 140-character increments on the Twitterbox.

SPREADING THE GOSPEL OF *NOT*-SPELL

Johnny B. Goode is not into *everything*. You name it and you're into it? He's not. Mention a band? Never heard of it. Mention a cuisine? Never tried it and has no intention of doing so. Mention something you're absolutely one thousand and one-half percent sure he's heard of? Fail with ranch sauce. Other people would act sheepish about their ignorance, ask to hear more details, or feign a promise to experience whatever it is in the future. Not Johnny B. Goode. He cultivates and jealously guards his ignorance, which he views as a sign of good taste and high culture. You know who also does that? People who believe in ear candling, libertarianism, and "bodily humors."

BEING AN UNWILLING SPECTACLE

Johnny B. Goode loves to place himself somewhere in public and then do something a passerby can't help but comment on. Examples include drawing primitive patterns on the sidewalk with chalk, knitting abstract shapes, collecting found objects and assembling them into impromptu art pieces, or assembling ham radios. He'll then act slightly annoyed at you for asking him about it. "Yes, I am stacking empty cream of mushroom soup cans in front of an abortion clinic... *Why?* Well, why not?" He'll follow with a cryptic smile and go back to his labors, only to lament in a café shortly after that, "People in this town don't get my art." Another way this manifests itself is in his dress and grooming. Why grow eighteenth-century facial hair and spends hours each day in front of the mirror with an eyebrow comb and mustache wax if you don't want anyone to notice? Privacy is easily obtained, son. Just grab some JCPenney separates and dress like everyone else.

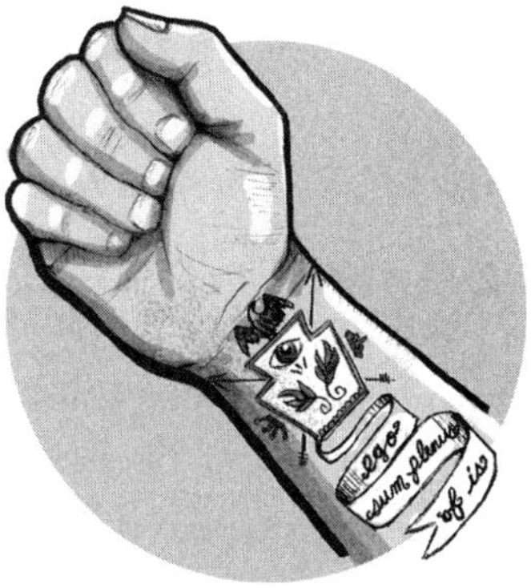

His Wardrobe

aka Proper & Improper Attire . . .

Fig. 2b: Johnny B. Goode acts like his ink don't stink.

TASTE THE NEUTRAL RAINBOW

A lot of thought goes into Johnny B. Goode's wardrobe. It always has, even when he was in middle school. On picture day, he was the only third-grader wearing a striped shirt instead of the private school–requested solids. Later, when he went off to university and realized *everyone* was wearing outlandish clothes, he flipped the other way around. His reasoning? College is such a predictable place to nonconform.

Johnny B. Goode

What He Wears

+ **Earth tones:** Black is too artsy-fartsy, and brights are for misguided teenagers and LA residents trying too hard. He wants clothing that whispers: "Enjoy your satanic Pizza Hut, fascists. I will sip water and eat this soy-germ bar." Forest green is also handy for hiding the sweat stains from his crystal rock deodorant, which doesn't actually work.
+ **Stuff from another place and time:** Russian messenger bags, Japanese snow boots, old hats from the Civil War. Before you met, you thought it was really cute. Now that you're dating, you wish he would stop. There's no need to dress that way when you're going to the hardware store to pick up shower caulk.
+ **Messaging:** On T-shirts, shoe soles, the back of his hand, the outside of his jacket, his guitar case, and his cubicle at work. Anything that's near his person gets covered in slogans. They're either extremely graphic (e.g., "Minks scream at 43 decibels when their pelts are removed, the same as that of a three-year-old child") or nonsensical (e.g., "No one is free when freedom loses art").
+ **A tattoo he won't tell you about:** It looks like a bird crossed with a sitar, but there's something vaguely nautical and what looks like a Latin quote? The truth is more boring than you will ever conceive of and involves a friend's older brother's band and a trip on mushrooms. Unless you're a masochist, we advise you not to ask him about it.

Every Rose Has Its Thorn

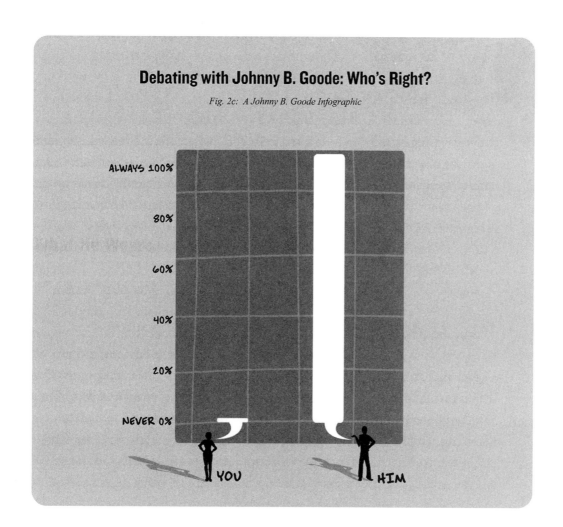

How to Get Backstage

or at the Very Least His Phone Number...

Fig 2d: Johnny B. Goode's dog is uncut, is free-range, volunteers with the blind, and eats an organic raw diet from a Fair Trade bamboo dish.

APPEAR IN PUBLIC WITH A BIG, DORKY PROP

Suggestions include a three-legged rescue dog, a huge tote bag full of library books with a grieving sparrow embroidered on the front, or materials for a found art project: a stack of vintage pornography and a rotting wheelbarrow. Hit the nearest artsy neighborhood and then take your prop for a little walk. Alternatively, you can drag it behind you, pausing every so often to dab the sweat from your brow with an antique handkerchief, and draw attention to your struggle.

Why It Works

Johnny B. Goode is lazy about talking to girls (read: terrified), and this gives him a great opener. Just know that for the first twenty minutes, Johnny B. Goode will more likely appear interested in the quirky item rather than in you, yourself. You could be standing there naked as a jaybird, and he won't notice. Don't let it deter you. He'll eventually wise up.

BROADCAST YOUR LOVE OF REAL OR PRETEND FOREIGN TRAVEL

Order salad *after* your main course. Instead of Captain Morgan's, ask for vodka in your Coke the next time you're at the bar. Cultivate an expression of detached bemusement. Carry chopsticks in your purse, along with a waterproof compass. Celebrate obscure holidays in a public fashion. Skip out of work early to watch the World Cup and wear one of those huge weird scarves.

Why It Works

Johnny B. Goode idealizes all things foreign, including girls, all the while overlooking much of the awesomeness that goes on in his own backyard. This is a guy who's never eaten a funnel cake or witnessed a demolition derby. Our hearts fill with sorrow. Now, it's a known fact that it's really difficult to become a visiting Latvian/Brazilian/Asian, etc., if you weren't already born one. The next-best thing is to be a woman who loves foreign travel. Throw out something like "This would *never* be a problem in Kabul," and Johnny B. Goode is *en el amor, ma petite courgette*.

GET POLITICAL ON A SOCIAL NETWORK

First, stalk Johnny B. Goode's social networking profiles and determine a way to get your posts and updates read by your target audience (i.e., Johnny B. Goode). This may require befriending someone who sends out online petitions every thirty-six seconds or feigning an interest in Bono. It'll be worth it. Trust us. Next, post a link to an obscure but controversial article, video, or story. Try BBC or NPR. Even CNN will work, as long as you're making fun of it.

Why It Works

While all Johnny B. Goodes consider themselves activists, only a small proportion are 100 percent full-time active about it. Passive activism is where it's at with these guys. They genuinely believe their blog updates are changing minds and shaping human history as it unfolds. Johnny B. Goode will respond to your post because he's interested in women who are "renegades" and "iconoclasts" just like himself. You don't have to tell him that you don't give a shit about that particular subject. You can always fix the karma by volunteering or donating to the cause of your choice later on. For now, enjoy the booty.

PLAYLIST

If I Had a Hammer (I'd Trade It for Something Less Violent): Johnny B. Goode's Favorite Protest Songs

1. **"What's Going On"—Marvin Gaye, 1970, Motown**
   This 1970s consciousness-raising hit is best listened to on pot. Unfortunately, it's ruined when Johnny B. Goode talks over it. Yeah, yeah, yeah, *The Autobiography of Malcolm X* was a mind-blower. You going to pass that shit or what?

2. **"Man in Black"—Johnny Cash, 1971, Columbia Records**
   Cash is the only country artist deemed worthy enough for Johnny B. Goode's "diverse" musical collection of college-educated white males. He listens to this antiwar anthem while wearing his one and only belt buckle.
3. **"Sunday Bloody Sunday"—U2, 1983, Island**
   Johnny B. Goode was so moved by this lyrical account of factional violence in Northern Island, he went on to skim not one but *three* Wikipedia articles.
4. **"Out of Step"—Minor Threat, 1983, Dischord**
   Johnny B. Goode was so straight edge during high school that instead of having a stick up his ass, he had a sustainable-wood ruler. Then he went to college, discovered that booze and girls are fun, and moved this one to the Archive file.
5. **"Battle Hymn of the Republic"—Julia Ward Howe, 1862**
   Johnny B. Goode's great-great-grandfather thought the Abolitionists were cool. Then they got an engraving in *The Atlantic Monthly* and thought they were hot porridge just because the Supervisory Committee for Recruiting Colored Regiments in Philadelphia gave them their backing. After that, he gave away his sheet music. Fucking sellouts.

POP QUIZ

Meme a Little Meme: How Well Do You Know Johnny B. Goode?

A meme (rhymes with *dream* or "Bumble and Bumble Men's Ultra-Luxe Pomade and Finishing Crème") is an idea that gets passed around from person to person. Sometimes it's funny; most of the time it's super-lame, like a "Ten Reasons Why Spanx Are Better Than Men" forward.

Johnny B. Goode is far too cool for such bandwagon amusements, so that's why we're going to make you do it for him. Fill out this quiz like your Johnny B. Goode would, and see if he's the real deal or a hopeless poser.

1. Who is the last person he talked to?
    a. His friend
    b. His girlfriend
    c. His boss
    d. Himself. He keeps an audio journal on his iPhone.

2. What is he doing right now?
    a. Listening to music
    b. Eating
    c. Working
    d. Silk-screening images of antique dentures onto recycled cardboard

3. What did he dream last night?
    a. He was late.
    b. He was naked.
    c. He was having sex.
    d. He was being verbally shamed by BrooklynVegan commenters.

4. Does he have any pet peeves?
    a. People who don't tip, pushy drivers
    b. Yappy dogs, loud neighbors
    c. Double-dippers, daytime talk shows
    d. He doesn't have any. He thinks anger is a false construct.

5. What is his favorite pizza topping?
    a. Pepperoni
    b. Sausage
    c. Green peppers
    d. Dandelion greens

6. What is his favorite TV show?
    a. Anything on MTV, VH1, or Bravo
    b. *Law & Order,* most crime dramas
    c. *National Geographic* or nature shows
    d. Have you read *Television: The Worst Thing Ever*? No? He's got it right here on his Kindle.

7. **Favorite celebrity?**
   a. Megan Fox
   b. Blake Lively
   c. Taylor Swift
   d. Celebrity? Sorry, you're going to have to explain that one to him.

SCORING

MOSTLY D'S = JOHNNY B. GOODE
You smell that? It's a Johnny B. Goode plug-in. Scent: Unwarranted Tropical Snobbery. Let it wash over you as you relax into a splintery chair made from recycled lumber, eyes half closed as you listen to a lecture on the erosion of online privacy and ponder your future with a less talented male version of Yoko Ono.

MOSTLY EVERYTHING ELSE = JOHNNY B. NOTHING
He's a glassblower, a Republican, the one who always sneezes in the egg salad at the Teddy Bear Picnic, or maybe the boy next door. Whatever he is, he's certainly not a Johnny B. Goode. (Sigh. Eye roll.)

IF YOU DECIDE TO BOOK HIM FOR ONE NIGHT ONLY

aka the Ins and Outs of Being Friends with Benefits . . .

 *The Pros*

HE'S RESPONSIBLE

He's more sex-educated than most sex educators and he's respectful of your reproductive views, whether you're pro-life, pro-choice, or pro-I-don't-know. No one has to talk this guy into taking precautions, although he may insist on using soy-based non-animal-tested lube and free-range vegan condoms. If that makes you uncomfortable, just mention that *you* know of a friend who wound up with a vegan baby after using the aforementioned form of protection, and he'll quickly come around.

HE WON'T GET ALL STUPID PORNO

The vast majority of Johnny B. Goodes watch adult movies. (Is 2:14 seconds of something considered a movie? Should we say "clip"? "Artistic short"?) However, unlike some other guys, Johnny B. Goode doesn't take his cues from them. This is partly because he thinks flipping someone around and folding them like a Krazy Straw and shouting, "That's right, take it!" is stupid and partly because he doesn't want to be found out. He can't admit to being sexually stimulated by spray-tanned nineteen-year-olds who couldn't cut it at community college. He's far too snobbish. To this your joints say, "Thank you, kind sir."

HE'S GOOD AT THE SLOW JAMS

You want to know what heaven is? Johnny B. Goode + an Indian-summer evening + clean crisp sheets + sappy alt country. Here's a guy who can "make love" without it resulting in a contractual obligation or being all cloying and emo. He'll look deeply into your eyes while doing it, and afterward you'll fall asleep in his ancient Pearl Jam shirt. It's this faux deep meaning–fraught experience, and the best part is he doesn't pester you with a bunch of needy "When can I see you again?" texts the following morning.

The Cons

HE'S NOT OPEN TO SUGGESTION

As much as Johnny B. Goode wants to bypass the uncaring male stereotype of the 2-Pump-Chump, he wants to get his way even more. When you ask for something off the usual menu, whether it's a much-deserved spanking or a quickie on the kitchen counter, Johnny B. Goode will often respond by claiming fatigue or saying he's not into it. It doesn't matter whether the request is small (let's use a vibe) or big (let's get a third), Johnny B. Goode doesn't like being told what to do. A shame, because as girl power as he is, he'd make an awesome sub.

HE'S BEEN POORLY TRAINED

Johnny B. Goode tends to favor shy, quiet types, though he pays extensive lip service to preferring loud, mouthy girls. When he actually hooks up with one (that would be you, my darling), he is shocked to discover that someone is questioning his techniques and motives. Example 1: *What do you mean, you want to come? Oh well. Okay. If you have to. But can you be quick about it? I've got to get to the co-op before it closes. . . .* Example 2: *My tongue is tired. Can we just spoon?* No, Johnny B. Goode. We cannot.

HE CAN'T PLAY THROUGH

There are some guys who could fuck through a nuclear event. Homeless people could pelt them with cans of soda pop and they wouldn't slow their roll. Sadly, Johnny B. Goode is like the princess and the penis: He can fuck only if conditions are *perfect*. Problem is, they never are. The sheets smell funny. The cat's making him sneeze. Your roommate's home. He ate too much battered cod. It's always something, and for a fuck friend, it's a lot to put up with, especially when you know that finding a replacement is rarely that difficult.

IF YOU DECIDE TO MAKE HIM THE HOUSE BAND

aka from Groupie to Girlfriend and Beyond . . .

 *The Pros*

HE MAKES YOU WANT TO BE A BETTER MAN . . . ER, WO-MAN

For as much as we make fun of him, Johnny B. Goode is (duh) good. He may put his kung fu slipper in his mouth and act like a grouch on occasion, but on the whole he means well. Whereas other guys may drag you down, Johnny B. Goode will lift you up. You will be more virtuous by looking at your own virtuousness (or lack thereof) beside him. Stick with him, and you'll actually volunteer instead of signing up for the meetings and then canceling because of something "very important," like an *Arrested Development* marathon. If anyone is going to help you fulfill your daydream of moving to the country and having little Pilates babies and raising alpacas, it's this one.

HE GIVES GOOD BIO

You can introduce Johnny B. Goode to a coworker, friend, relative, or person you haven't seen in ten years and they're bound to be impressed by something, whether it's his political beliefs, his intelligence, or his work with the impoverished. This is not like young guys, whose accomplishments you have to pad ("He's in Sandwich Artistry"), or distant guys, for whom you're filling in the vital stats because they're never around. Johnny B. Goode sounds like someone you should be with. As long as he can put on a thick-knit Irish sweater, coax his beard into a reasonable semblance of normal, and keep his fiery opinions to himself, you won't get any flak from Grandma and Grandpa.

HE ENCOURAGES BY EXAMPLE

There are only so many times you can tuck into a chocolate doughnut and a Marlboro while Johnny B. Goode sprinkles flaxseed into his oatmeal. Likewise, there's a limit on how believable it is when you can say "Just this once" as you get into your car and drive it to the other end of the strip mall parking lot because you can't be bothered to walk. Thrift, honesty, temperance, patience—these are all Johnny B. Goode values. He's like a Boy Scout, if they didn't get their kerchiefs in a bunch about letting in homosexuals. You've always wanted to practice what he preaches, and now you have the perfect role model.

The Cons

HE'S PREACHY

While Johnny B. Goode may be able to keep his opinions at bay if it's a friend-with-benefits situation or the early stages of couplehood, it won't be long before they come out. It's amazing how someone who shares so much of your worldview can still have so much to gripe about. You want a boyfriend, not a humorless C-SPAN commentator. Whatever happened to "Orange you glad I didn't say banana?" and knock-knock jokes? According to Johnny B. Goode, the former is cruel to migrant workers and the latter are insensitive to the deaf and homeless.

HE DOESN'T CHOOSE HIS BATTLES

Johnny B. Goode will contradict you and debate you and essentially just run you into the ground. He's great to bring to a dinner party and all your friends come up to you afterward to congratulate you on finding such an enlightened smarty-pants with such interesting opinions. You respond by offering to send him home with them. It's cool to be dating an activist, but it's not cool dealing with it 24/7. It's like living in a message board thread that never ends. You want to stop engaging, but he doesn't stop goading you. Just once you'd like to express a neutral statement, such as "We're out of soap," without his challenging the assertion.

HE'S SOMETIMES A DOUCHE IN LIBERAL CLOTHING

Just because someone's out to save the world doesn't mean the rest of the world will want to stay in it with him once he does. In fact, they're probably building a rocket ship to escape him right now. Sometimes it's better to be with someone who doesn't mirror all of your views but who's open-minded and able to get along with people. Someone respectful and down-to-earth. You were once set up with a philandering corporate lawyer (you didn't find out until after you were on the date), and even that guy was more polite and convivial. *How is that even possible?*

HOW TO END IT HARMONIOUSLY

WITH DISINTEREST

Johnny B. Goode needs tension the way living things need food, water, and shelter. Take away the epic debates, the ongoing disapproval, and the attempts to convert each other to your point of view, and you're left with very little. What will Johnny B. Goode do now that you're no longer embarrassed when he uses school bake sales as an opportunity to hand out homemade leaflets on animal cruelty? What would he do if you just smiled and let him lecture while you zoned out and thought about what you were going to have for a snack later? (By the way, go with the taco. It's still good.) We'll tell you: He'll give you some spiel about how you're not connecting (really? shock!) and some horseshit about needing a break. He thinks it's temporary. You make sure it's not.

WITH A SWEATSHOP-FREE DRESSING DOWN

Johnny B. Goode is a hypocrite, like 100 percent of the entire waking world. You're not bothered by it, but to Johnny B. Goode hypocrisy is the worst sin ever. Ask him to give you an estimate of how much jet fuel he burned during his globe-trotting sojourns. Ask him if he's kept in touch with the kids he helped during that five-day trip to Brazil and if they're still getting fed on an ongoing basis. Don't do it in a spiteful way. It should all seem very innocent. Before you know it, Johnny B. Goode will be good and cranky. He'll be picking fights and heading down that rocky road to Breakupville (a locally built, sustainable community, founded 2010).

WITH YOUR NOT-SO-BEST SELF

Now's the time where we go all Seinfeld and feel compelled to follow with "Not that there's anything *wrong* with that." It's just that Johnny B. Goodes fall in love with ideas and concepts, not people. They don't believe in flaws or missteps or mistakes or losing control of oneself. They feel that everything has a greater purpose, that even the barfing they did after a night of pale ales was a form of "intestinal cleansing." When you let him see you in all your imperfection, you're doing both of yourselves a favor. You're freeing yourself to be who you really are, and you're freeing him to find someone else who will also fail to measure up to his insane standards. *Que será*.

HOW TO KEEP MAKING SWEET MUSIC TOGETHER

LEARN WHEN RIGHT IS WRONG

Johnny B. Goode is a stickler for detail and a constant corrector. Naturally, this will chafe at you after a while. You get so sick of corrections that you pick up on his corrections and start correcting him. Now we've got two people, one a professional, the other a newcomer, both trying to outcorrect each other. Sounds like a real ball. In order to preserve your happiness as a couple, learn how to pick your battles. Not only that, but where to stage them, i.e., at home in private versus at dinner in front of another couple. You can let him think that he has the correct Death Cab for Cutie lyrics (he doesn't) or you can hold firm on this earth-shattering debate and be miserable.

YOU CAN HAVE FUN AND HE DOESN'T HAVE TO BE THERE

Real fun. Easy fun. Not the slow-cooked kind with twee handicrafts and five-mile-long hikes and academic book swaps. Perhaps you like all of the latter, but if you do, you know all too well by now that Johnny B. Goode does not. Whatever's your pleasure, get out there and do it. Don't get so enmeshed that you no longer spend any leisure time solo. It's fun at first, having a partner for Hair Metal Bingo. However, after multiple Wednesdays of your partner rolling his eyes and pretending he's never heard of Bon Jovi, wouldn't it be better to have a new bingo partner, one who screams like a baby eagle every time the caller says "Richie Sambora"? Yes, we know that some activities are more fun when

 Every Rose Has Its Thorn

you do them as a couple. We'd also like to dress like Zooey Deschanel in wacky hats without looking like we're escapees from a group home, but we can't have everything we want and you can't, either.

PRINCIPLES RESPECT PRINCIPLES

Learn to put your foot down. Even if that foot is clad in mainstream indie-cool Converse mass-produced in China. Can't bend on a particular political issue, personal quirk, or brand of toothpaste you've been using since you were a child? Then don't. Reinforce it consistently and without apology, and Johnny B. Goode will eventually come to respect you for it. He may even start to be more open about his own inconsistencies and hypocrisies. The proverbial cracks in the cool sensitive-guy armor will start to show. Each one that appears—Did you know that he has *Baywatch* Season 1 in his Netflix queue?—will make you love him a little more.

FOR THE RECORD

aka Relationship Lessons from the School of Rock . . .

AFTER-SCHOOL-SPECIAL SYNDROME CAN BE CURED

You know the drill. The child tries (unsuccessfully) to live up to her best friend or older sister whom everyone admires: "I can never be as good as Suzy! I'm worthless! Why even bother?" Here's the deal, though: While Johnny B. Goode is hip, well dressed, Zenlike and morally/socially responsible, he's even better at letting everyone know it. It's all a bunch of nontoxic smoke and free-trade mirrors. Ask around. At least six out of ten people will probably concur that he's kind of a dillhole. You're not—an achievement to be proud of.

THE INTERNET ISN'T ALWAYS YOUR FRIEND

Johnny B. Goode will always include you on his e-mail petition and benefit show forwards, no matter how bloody the breakup. This feels inappropriate, considering that last time you saw him, you were both snotting and crying your eyes out. Through the process of Google-stalking, you'll find that Johnny B. Goode has something to say about everything, and he writes about it all on his various Facebook, blog, and Twitter accounts: parrots as pets, health care, Brooke Hogan. But nothing about the relationship that has taken up his existence for the past eighteen months. Our advice? Get familiar with the "defriend" and "unsubscribe" buttons. They're better than Prozac.

RULES ARE BENDY

You have become used to living under many of Johnny B. Goode's mandates, more or less because as a kind, socially conscious, and enlightened person, you agree with them. However, it takes a big man to rewash Ziploc bags but a fun man to throw one in the trash after relieving it of pot. Johnny B. Goode would be proud of this grassroots-level disobedience if he weren't against all it stood for. Go ahead. Watch *The Fast and the Furious*. Stop trying to be all *Masterpiece Theatre*. There are certain times in life where you're allowed unlimited vodka and chicken tenders.

★★★ Reviews

What Critics Are Saying About Johnny B. Goode

"He was so many more degrees better than me. You'd hang a picture and it was not straight. Everything he did was better than everyone else. He didn't think of himself as high and mighty, but he definitely came off that way."

—Alison

"He was a vegan. He also didn't believe in sex. We were together for six months. He wound up being a heroin addict, which I didn't know when I first met him. He was in college studying shit that didn't matter. Now he works for the government."

—Amy

"He wasn't good. But he was too good for everyone else. My writing was too commercial. The books I read weren't literary enough. We weren't allowed to go to Starbucks. McDonald's was the garbage dump. When it was convenient for him to like mainstream things, then he liked them."

—Nicole

YOUR MINI PRESS KIT

Johnny B. Goode is the guy who . . .

- Purchases vegan Pirate's Booty with a World Wildlife Fund credit card and then feels naughty for eating "junk food."

- Lectures you when you look at porn.

- Tries to sell you on extra virgin olive oil as a lubricant.

- Believes having spent a parent-funded semester abroad makes him better than you.

- Brews his own mouthwash.

- Uses "I don't watch TV" as his default response to any cultural reference, getting flustered when the topic of conversation turns out to be a book.

SEXY MOTHER

THE MEET & GREET

Who He Is

A Picasso of the penis. The best thing to happen to women since the invention of the tampon. A sex bomb that's been doused with pheromones and set on fire. The adventurous, worldly gourmet of the bedroom. Many guys enjoy oral sex, but few of them can identify a former girlfriend in the dark by her vagina's "flavor profile."

What He's All About

Great sex you find every few years. A Sexy Motherfucker you find once in a lifetime. Which is probably for the best, considering how many marathon runners die sooner than other people. Anything that intense can't be good for your body. While sex addicts engage in damaging, compulsive behavior they cannot control, sex is so deeply ingrained in this guy's everyday behavior that it's like saying, "I'm addicted to breathing air through my lungs," or "I'm addicted to being upright and mobile." When he's not fucking your brains out, Sexy Motherfucker is one of the most enlightened, self-confident-without-being-a-douche-about-it guys around. He treats you with a surprising amount of respect for someone who can turn around and slap your ass and instruct you to "gag on it" (which you're all too willing to do).

PERSONAL MOTTO

Always open.

Turn-ons

Doing it in public, doing it in private, the state map of Florida, tacos, hot dogs, "Fuck me" pumps, "Fuck me" Birkenstocks, your female friends, your male friends, mahjong.

Turnoffs

None.

THE HEADLINERS

Here are three music icons, chosen not only for their throbbing pulchritude but also for their ability to invoke a trancelike swooning and surrender among women, the effects of which are similar to a high-grade neurotoxin at a Mississippi gospel revival.

Let's start with the only living human who doesn't look fat in white spandex overalls, move on to a sexy New Waver with two personas in one body, and close with ninety-five pounds of purple passion from America's heartland.

MICK JAGGER

Who He Is
Rolling Stones front man, Keith Richards's codependent and domestic life partner, pioneer in the field of awkward dance, lips and hips, Queen Elizabeth's sexiest knight.

What Makes Him Such a Sexy Motherfucker
Posed and postured and made lewd lip contortions in a time when wearing a sweater vest without a dickey was considered the pinnacle of wild. Forty years later, his shaggy hairdo and self-satisfied chicken strut still bring female audience members to musical climax.

> "I don't expect Mick to just pray to God while on tour."
>
> Bianca Jagger, Mick's first wife, *People*, June 9, 1975

Sexy Motherfucker Highlights
- Was famously asked to change lyrics of "Let's Spend the Night Together" for *The Ed Sullivan Show*. Mick went along, but rolled his eyes so defiantly that the words were even more lurid in the process.
- Father of seven children. By four different mamas.
- According to legend, was once found naked in bed with David Bowie. Both camps claim it was innocent. Just two dudes being dudes, naked as the day is long, and tuckered out from a long night of rock 'n' roll. Guy on guy? *Hot*. Guy on guy where both guys kind of look like girls? *Thank you, Jesus H. Santa Claus.*

DAVID BOWIE

Who He Is
Ziggy Stardust's real dad, New Wave and glam rock icon, "Little Drummer Boy" Bing Crosby duet partner, eye makeup maven, primary reason why the seventies got so weird.

What Makes Him Such a Sexy Motherfucker
Nordic god good looks. A voice like a horror movie narrator. Vulnerability, creative genius, and impeccable fashion sense. Looks like he might have evil powers.

> **Sexy Motherfucker Highlights**
> - The Mick Jagger incident (see above).
> - Managed to look scorching in Jim Henson's movie *Labyrinth*, despite the mullet and nipple-high jodhpurs.
> - Model wife Iman admitted in an online fan forum that she and David occasionally paint each other's toenails.

"When I was fourteen, sex suddenly became all-important to me. It didn't really matter who or what it was with, as long as it was a sexual experience."

David Bowie,
Playboy,
September 1976

Every Rose Has Its Thorn

PRINCE

Who He Is
American musician, songwriter, and record producer; name-changing pain in the ass; Morris Day fictional nemesis; Apollonia wrangler; lace and velvet importer.

What Makes Him Such a Sexy Motherfucker
A thousand-yard stare. Facial expressions capable of removing panties through a television screen and a voice known to induce pregnancy through a stereo. Prince doesn't ask; he takes. Then he sends a trembling flunky out to hand you the purple paper bill.

> "People say I'm wearing heels because I'm short. I wear heels because the women like 'em."
>
> Prince,
> *Rolling Stone*,
> September 12, 1985

Sexy Motherfucker Highlights
- Doesn't sing so much as shriek, whine, moan, and purr.
- Walks around dressed like a gay leather daddy who got lost in a French fabric store.
- Conquests include Carmen Electra, Sheena Easton, Vanity of Vanity 6 (an all-female '80s group that performed in lingerie and which, shockingly, he founded), and Bangles lead singer Susanna Hoffs. To save time, let's just say everyone. You can write in if you want your name removed, and it'll be in the next edition, with the footnotes.

His Regular Venues
aka Where You'll Find Him . . .

AT DRUGSTORES AND COSMETICS COUNTERS
Sexy Motherfucker is about looking, feeling, and smelling good and is confident enough in his masculinity (and who wouldn't be, with all the ass he's getting?) to bend a couple of gender rules. You first spot him in the beauty supply store, where he's trying to decide between two shades of hair color. He invites you out for the next night to see the result. Later that evening, you get to see how well the carpet matches the new drapes. That's assuming, of course, there's carpet there at all.

PLACES WHERE PEOPLE ARE MINIMALLY CLOTHED
Think less swinger's club and more Burning Man encampment, nude bicycle ride, or burlesque-themed "fashion show." Sexy Motherfucker is totally comfortable with his body and can't imagine what it's like to not want your junk revealed to large groups of people. You are at a swank hotel pool party sucking down vodka sodas and repeating the Queen Latifah mantras you prepared the night before—"I am a strong black woman, I am a strong black woman." (Fun fact: You do this even if you are are a scrawny Caucasian.) You gaze at Sexy Motherfucker's strutting perfection in envy, and to your surprise, you find him approaching.

Every Rose Has Its Thorn

ANYWHERE HE CAN BE THE CENTER OF FEMALE ATTENTION

Sexy Motherfucker is always down for female company, whether that means being the sole male in the craft circle or the only one who has to worry about getting a sweaty ball sac at Bikram yoga. Lest you mistake him for a womanizing opportunist sissy with a pirate blouse and glue-on ponytail, might I remind you that these are activities Sexy Motherfucker *genuinely likes to do*. He's also known to attract females by engaging in outdoor manual labor, always winding up on the "skins" team in whatever pickup game he's playing, and—the most obvious girl-attracter of all—playing music. Those microphone-fellating lips and bass-caressing fingers are enough to win over even the most "Been there, done that," huge-yawn anti-groupie of groupies.

His Act

aka Ways of Working the Crowd . . .

APPEARING LANGUID

Sexy Motherfucker could be in a chemo chair, awaiting execution, or on a subway car in downtown Tokyo, the kind where uniformed men with sticks cram you into the train, and he'll still look relaxed and calm. He doesn't sit on chairs; he molests them. He makes 1960s spaghetti-western clichés come to life as he saunters through doorways and leans with one boot up against the wall. Every move is calculated to not look calculated, every yawn and stretch combo a *Playgirl* centerfold. With this is an air of calm confidence and a subtle psychological message: "Come pet me, I am harmless!" like when a cat sprawls out. Even though you're wickedly allergic and you're going to hate yourself later, you can't help giving the little guy a belly rub along with your phone number.

TALKING TO THE PERSON WITH THE MOST SOCIAL CURRENCY

It might be the DJ, the bartender, the guy manning the grill at the outdoor barbecue, or the lead singer of the band you just saw. Sexy Motherfucker knows just about everyone. Unlike your ex, he's got great connections but doesn't act like a jag about it. A breed apart from the social butterfly, Sexy Motherfucker tends to conduct his conversations one-on-one. You can't tell what the hell they're talking about, but it's driving you mad with curiosity.

PLAYING TALK-SHOW HOST, SEX EDUCATOR, AND REPORTER

Sexy Motherfucker is a collector of secret admissions, guilty confessions, and bawdy overshares. Less skilled peers marvel at his ability to ferret out a total stranger's spit/swallow preference within three minutes of meeting her at a bar. Part of it's that he looks too good to be not gay. If there's no chance of hooking up, then it's the same thing as girl talk, is it not? Another part of it is his approach: He's friendly, impartial, and not at all smarmy. He gives off the aura of someone who doesn't *need* to get laid, which—as cliché as it sounds—only makes you want him more. It's only when you're forty minutes into the discussion that's covered everything from your preferred masturbation tool (the Shower Massage™) to your creepy adolescent crush on your cousin that you realize that he's very *not gay*. The next thing you know, you're sharing a cab over to his place, all rarin' to go and riled up.

His Wardrobe

aka Proper & Improper Attire . . .

HEAVY PETTING

Sexy Motherfucker wears things other guys could never get away with: vanilla body spray, painted-on jeans, and teddy-bear-print high-tops, yet always manages to make it look like the most manly ensemble. He's also a big believer in texture: velvet, leather, mesh, cashmere. Coincidentally, the same kind of fabrics that drunk girls in bars like to touch.

Fig 3b:
Sexy Motherfucker looks better in your panties than you do.

What He Wears

- **Perfect Hair™.** The cut and color are so good they defy whatever hair standards you've set for male prospects: It's long if you hate hippies and red if you're turned off by British royals. The kind of hair that has you immediately imagining what it's like to run your pervy little mitts through it.
- **Tight pants.** Let other guys sag. Sexy Motherfucker prefers a constantly hugged groin region. When he got locked out of his house and had to wear his friend's basketball shorts, he was self-conscious and miserable. When his package isn't prominent it's like he's no longer himself.
- **Man jewelry.** Tons of it. But no tacky ID bracelets and chunky pinky rings here. Think little rope bracelets, delicate amulets, quirky stick pins and charms. He'll leave some of it when he spends the night, and you'll wear all of it 24/7, even in the shower.
- **Storybook pieces.** A leather jacket actually worn in *Easy Rider*, given to him by a friend who works in estate sales; his dad's chukka boots from the sixties in London; huge Chanel sunglasses he scored at a photo shoot. Is he a man, or a legend come to life?

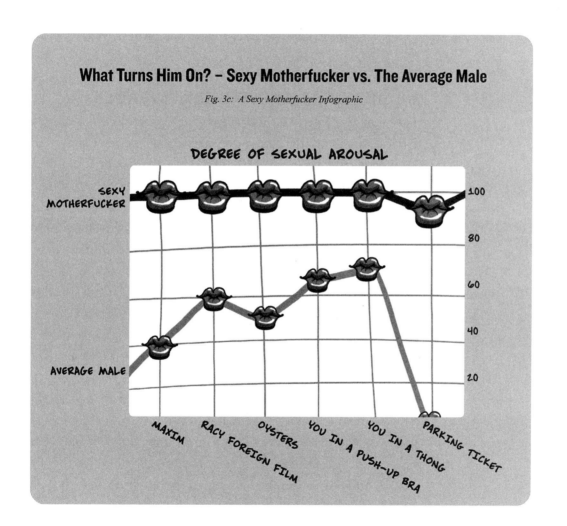

How to Get Backstage

or at the Very Least His Phone Number . . .

Fig 3d:
All Sexy Motherfucker needs is a signal . . .

BE UNAWARE AND/OR UNAVAILABLE

You never meet a Sexy Motherfucker when you're looking your best. No, that'd be too easy and logical. It's only when you haven't showered in four days and you're patting your hair with brown eye shadow in an attempt to absorb the grease and rubbing a Magic Tree under your pits before going out that he'll materialize—seemingly out of nowhere—and approach you. Same goes for when you're consoling a friend whose aunt just died and breaking focus to flirt with the hot guy who sits down at your table would be the ultimate in inappropriate. Are you not at all prepared to meet someone or not simply interested in meeting someone even if someone good *did* come along? Then relax; your pickup is assured.

Why It Works

Sexy Motherfucker likes a challenge. Not in a predatory sort of way. He's just fascinated by a woman who doesn't immediately try to fuck him. Of course you *do* want to fuck him, you just didn't realize it until now. Still, let him remain under that impression for a little while longer. He'll want to be like the aliens in that one movie and take you up in his spaceship and study you. It will, of course, require some nudity on your part. You're okay with that, aren't you?

Every Rose Has Its Thorn

OVULATE

That is, produce and discharge eggs from an ovary or ovarian follicle. This comes naturally for most of us, but if it's that time of month or you no longer hang with Aunt Flow, you can simulate the effect by wearing the same underpants for a couple of days or rubbing one out right before you go out. Works better than the best perfume.

Why It Works

Sexy Motherfuckers are intrinsically tuned in to women. They're like those dogs that come up and nuzzle your crotch while you're at a classy dinner party. You know what's up, the host knows what's up, the guests know what's up, and the whole thing's pretty fucking embarrassing. You might as well give Fido a few pets (and Sexy Motherfucker, while you're at it), because both of them are going to wind up humping your leg regardless.

TREAT HIM LIKE A REGULAR PERSON

Remind yourself that despite looking like a Greek god come to life, this guy poops, buys toothpaste, pays taxes, Googles exes, and does everything else normal humans do. Don't put him up on a pedestal, but don't be a faux bitch, either. If he's being a dick, call him on it. If he's cool to you, be cool.

Why It Works

Sexy Motherfucker thrives on female validation. It's pretty much the basis of his entire identity, so don't let his cock-of-the-walk bravado fool you. Compliment him on something other than his penis and watch him light up like Vegas on New Year's. A philosopher we're too lazy to look up once said something about how if you want to get laid, tell smart women they're hot and hot women they're smart. Reverse the genders and it's still true.

PLAYLIST

One-Eyed Monsters Have No Ears: Mood-Killing Songs Successfully Conquered by Sexy Motherfucker

1. **"In the Ghetto"—Elvis Presley, 1969, RCA**
   Oh, *that's* what was playing? Weird. He didn't notice.
2. **"Animal Crackers in My Soup"—Shirley Temple, 1935, EMI**
   Oh, *that's* what was playing? Weird. He didn't notice.
3. **"Theme from Jaws"—John Williams, 1975, Decca**
   Oh, *that's* what was playing? Weird. He didn't notice.
4. **"Man! I Feel Like a Woman!"—Shania Twain, 1997, Mercury Nashville**
   Oh, *that's* what was playing? Weird. He didn't notice.
5. **"Turning Japanese"—The Vapors, 1980, United Artists**
   Oh, *that's* what was playing? Weird. He didn't notice.

POP QUIZ

Sexy Motherfucker Sex Ed 101

Is he a Sexy Motherfucker or just a fucker? Answer these seven questions and soon you'll know. And knowing is half the battle. The other half is reviving tired '80s cartoon references.

1. You're on vacation when Sexy Motherfucker gets accosted by a two-novelty-drinks-away-from-rapey bachelorette party. He reacts by:
   a. Smiling and waving with his free hand as he continues fingering you under the bar table.
   b. Ignoring you, flirting with them, and buying them a round of cosmos. Whoops, forgot yours.

2. Role-play:
   a. You were skeptical, but he's so good you find yourself raiding post-Halloween sales for cheerleader skirts, ski masks, and mechanic's jumpers.
   b. While playing doctor, he leapt up mid-coitus because he forgot to record the *House* season finale on the DVR.

3. He gives you orgasms:
   a. So good you want to film them and send the video to your ex-boyfriends, first boss, and the smug girl in grammar school who never shared her Fruit Roll-Up.
   b. Occasionally, but always whines that you take too long. You're pretty sure the multiorgasmic ex he's always bringing up as a point of comparison is a blow-up doll.

4. When sleeping over he makes his mark:
   a. On the sheets, in the form of cum stains. His and yours. Who knew?
   b. On your person, in the form of a nasty bruise when you trip on the shoes he left out in the hall. He waits a good five minutes after hearing you bite it before getting off the phone.

5. You go to a friend's wedding. He:
   a. Keeps sneaking you back to your guest suite for some mid-wedding breaks. You now have a shit-eating grin in all the bridal party pictures.
   b. Gets shit-faced and tries to hook up with the youngest bridesmaid while you're in the bathroom scrubbing out the chicken parm he spilled on your party gown.

6. Behind your back, your friends are most likely to call him:
   a. Sexpants, Hot Rod, Fun Buns.
   b. Turkeyface, Weaseldick. Señor Jerkoff, Ol' Droopy Balls.

(continued)

SCORING

MOSTLY A'S = SEXY MOTHERFUCKER
Congrats! You've got yourself a live one. Hope you've stocked up on cranberry juice for all those UTIs in your future.

MOSTLY B'S = FUCKER
Bad personalities can sometimes be saved by good sex. Bad sex can be saved by good personalities. This guy has neither. Dump him.

IF YOU DECIDE TO BOOK HIM FOR ONE NIGHT ONLY

aka the Ins and Outs of Being Friends with Benefits . . .

 *The Pros*

HE'S GOOD, REALLY GOOD

"Astounding!" says the *Los Angeles Times*. "I didn't know I could make noises like a meth-addled howler monkey on microphone feedback!" writes the *Boston Review*. Why is it so good? The man has skills, both mind and body. He's open-

 Every Rose Has Its Thorn

minded and experienced and can help you figure out what you like, even if you're not sure what that is, exactly. He's like a brilliant hairstylist: He knows when you want the same-old same-old and when you're ready to try something new. And just like that guy with the scissors, he's a once-in-a-lifetime find who always leaves you feeling kickass and beautiful.

HE'S SAFE

About condoms, about hygiene, about getting tested. He's so strict that he went to the 7-Eleven on a five a.m. condom run, even though you—in a ridiculously dangerous move that could only be the result of drinking to the point of near blackout—told him it was "just fine" and that he could "pull out." Luckily, Sexy Motherfucker knew not to trust anything that comes out of the mouth of the girl who just knocked over her highball glass and wandered into the kitchen he shares with his male roommates naked from the waist down in search of oyster crackers.

HE'S HAPPY WITH HIS STATION

Any Human Resources manager will tell you that one of the most difficult positions to fill is that of the front desk person. Even though many of the job duties aren't that complex—making copies, answering the phone, etc.—it's of critical importance and there tends to be high turnover. You need someone enthusiastic and competent, yet without other aspirations. Same with a fuck buddy, and that's why Sexy Motherfucker is *perfect*. He does not want to be *your* boyfriend. He does not want to be *anybody's* boyfriend, so there's little danger of his being poached by an outside recruiter.

Sexy Motherfucker

 ## The Cons

HE'S BAD WITH EMOTIONAL RESTRAINT

On certain days, at certain times, Sexy Motherfucker can act a little too boyfriend-like, and it's confusing. If he's had a tough day, he may start making plans for three months from now or just be extra cuddly. For the love of Ron Jeremy, Sexy Motherfucker, quit with your flip-flopping. Sex hormones are kissing cousins of love hormones, and if you're not careful, your vagina conspires with your brain to make you start cultivating idiotic fantasies. You don't have time for this shit. You're working two jobs. You want no-strings sex, not a Harlequin novel.

HE'S ALWAYS THINKING OUTSIDE YOUR BOX

Let's say you do a sexy dance at a bar one night. Now that's all he talks about, that sexy dance and how he wants to see you do it again, only this time wearing no panties. So you comply. Then you spend all night having nightmares about cell phone pictures of your pink parts all over the Internet. You start to reminisce about past relationships when *you* were the pushing the boundaries—the wanton hussy. You seem to have fallen into this demure role, with him taking it further and you throwing your hands up like a 1950s girl in the bullet-point bra.

HE'S NOT SO DISCREET

Around roommates, in public, walking around the house after sex wearing only a tiny pair of boxer briefs. Granted, Sexy Motherfucker looks fantastic, but that's not the point. The point is, your roommates and neighbors would prefer not to see his dangly bits when, toothbrush in hand, he ambles through the living room and performs his morning regimen naked in front of the sliding glass door. Every time you try to talk to him about it he laughs and says you're too uptight. Who cares if the headboard's banging? What does it matter if the whole house smells like sex when your parents come to visit? You do.

IF YOU DECIDE TO MAKE HIM THE HOUSE BAND

aka from Groupie to Girlfriend and Beyond . . .

 *The Pros*

YOU WON'T GET BORED IN BED
Add to that the closet. The laundry room. The church kitchen at the ladies auxiliary bake sale. You listen to your friends bitching about their dull sex lives and try to remain expressionless, but they always wind up calling you out anyway. Thanks to Sexy Motherfucker, you can breeze past articles in those shitty magazines you read at the doctor's office with inane titles like "1,001 Ways to

Put a Penis in a Vagina!" and "Take the ZZZ out of Getting Bizz-zeee" and move on to more important matters, like Kate Hudson's new boyfriend's ex-girlfriend and Robert Pattinson's favorite type of cereal.

YOU WON'T GET BORED OUT OF BED, EITHER

Sexy Motherfucker is spontaneous. He always picks up on and encourages your fledgling ideas and contributes suggestions of his own. You don't have to always make the decisions or man the controls. You hate the phrase because you've seen it abused so many times in the online personals, but Sexy Motherfucker has a true "passion for living," and you love being able to glom off it. Left to your own devices, you'd never leave the house, which makes it all the harder when you have to play cheerleader for someone else.

HE'S GOT HIS ACT TOGETHER

He looks good and lives well, whether it's the expensive cheese he has in his refrigerator, or the great relationship he has with his next-door neighbors. His work, social calendar, and familial relationships all seem to be on the right side of normal. He's got minor dramas, like anybody, but nothing insurmountable. You've been brainwashed to believe people who are this good at sex have enormous issues—like the stripper who cries tears of glitter each night as she hangs up her thong and reflects on her escape from a religious cult—but the longer you get to know Sexy Motherfucker, the more he disproves that notion.

 ## The Cons

HE'S PROBABLY NOT INTO MONOGAMY

In the rare instance he will commit (fresh out of a breakup, recent death in the family, more than three close friends getting married in the space of a year), he might start to act out after a while. It could be in the form of cheating. It could be increasingly active online friendships with attractive females. Not to excuse it, but Sexy Motherfucker doesn't do it because he's a dick or is out to conquer or manipulate women. He just likes sex and finds it really difficult to turn down that type of energy when it comes at him. You know that "I'd like to buy the world a Coke" advertising jingle? Replace the beverage with the act of intercourse.

HE'S HONEST TO A FAULT

You know everything about his past lovers, and he knows everything about yours. You appreciate the truth telling, but sometimes you really wish you could un-know what you just found out. When you make an offhand remark like "Yes, but you only have eyes for me, right?" he is quick to respond with a long lecture about how he doesn't believe in sexual jealousy, the Kinsey report, Freud, evolutionary biology, and ninety other kinds of yada yada. You understand and are well versed in the sexual revolution, but you were *making a joke*.

Sexy Motherfucker

HE TALKS OUT HIS ASS SOMETIMES

He likes to think of himself as more committed than he is. He stares at your boss's boobs at the office party because he's "a lover of beauty" and "very sensual," not because he's an oversexed horndog who can't control himself. How could you think that about him? Don't you believe him? He has a degree in comparative literature. He *is* capable of something deeper. Now, if you'll excuse him, he's got to go draw his friend nude. She's a visiting figure model and is going to sleep in his bed tonight, because the sheets on the guest bed are dirty and . . . why are you giving him that look?

HOW TO END IT HARMONIOUSLY

WITH A BANG

Breaking up immediately after screwing is rarely advisable. However, Sexy Motherfucker is in such a happy mood after sex that nothing's going to shake him out of it. He probably wouldn't even believe you. A half-hour after your last sex session, when you're glowy and sweaty, tell him you're going to be moving on. The positive for you is that you get one last fuck; the positive for him is that he gets to go out on a high note. Probably several high notes, as post-breakup sex will commence approximately five minutes after you pull the trigger. Hopefully you haven't met a new guy and double-booked.

 Every Rose Has Its Thorn

WITH A WHIMPER

Unlike some guys, Sexy Motherfucker responds well to the gradual fadeout. This is because, as nice as he is, he's self-absorbed. Get extra busy for a couple of weeks, then busier the next week and busier still the weeks that follow. Be polite and cordial in your blowoffs, lest you get the reverse-psychology boomerang effect of making him want you more. Casually mention that you're seeing someone off and on, per his non-monogamy mandate. Act blissful and happy, and he'll respond with blissful and happy. Once you're out of his sight, he'll use his fresh dumpee status as a tool to get even more tail.

WITH A WIRE MONKEY

During the late '50s and '60s neuroscientists and psychologists would separate baby primates from their mothers, which bummed the little guys out greatly. Researchers found that providing them with a facsimile of a mother, a wire form with some cloth attached to it, made the kids happy again. They just needed something, anything, to take the place of a warm body. Sexy Motherfucker needs this as well. Right after the breakup, introduce Sexy Motherfucker to a superhot friend or have him make a prearranged "surprise" cameo at a bachelorette party. He'll find a new place to store his banana in no time.

HOW TO KEEP MAKING SWEET MUSIC TOGETHER

GET USED TO THE ON SWITCH BEING ON
Like a dirtier version of the Olympic torch (originally carried by nude folks, who knew?), Sexy Motherfucker is always going to emit a sexual energy and look for the same in others. The upside? You get to do some flirting yourself. Which may not sound that appealing, especially if the relationship is on the new side and you're in the swoony first stages of love. To that we say, give it a couple of years. You just might find you're happy with the freedom his lecherousness allows you. And while other women are locked in sexless relationships, begging for it, you'll never have to deal with a dusty and neglected vagina.

YOU'RE NOT BEING GRADED ON IT
He may want to swing from the chandeliers every time you get naked, but that doesn't mean you have to comply. Go ahead and ask for plain old missionary. Tell him that period oral brings up a childhood fear of vampires. Some people are kinkier than others, and this isn't a contest. If it were, he'd always win, so there's no reason to pretend like you don't want to straight-up WASP-style some nights instead of breaking out the lube and the ass toys.

 Every Rose Has Its Thorn

LEAVE THE BEDROOM EVERY ONCE IN A WHILE

Get to know him in new ways. It may be weird at first, and you'll have to don your softest jeans because your ass is still a bit sore from the spanking and roleplay that took place last night, but you can learn a lot about a person by the way he behaves at a big-box store. Does he gravitate toward the huge jars of pretzel rods or the fifty-count box of Speed Stick in the personal care aisle? Does he gobble up the free samples like visiting royalty, or does he hover in the background like a shy little flower and wait for you to pass him a pig in a blanket? Building up the nonsexual aspects of your relationship is key to a long and happy coexistence with Sexy Motherfucker.

FOR THE RECORD

aka Relationship Lessons from the School of Rock . . .

BISEXUAL AND BEERSEXUAL ARE NOT EQUIVALENT

Now you will be able to say that you've engaged in a real, bona fide ménage à trois, complete with bullet vibe play and/or salad tossing. As opposed to, say, hyping up that one time you kissed a girl at a party and making it seem to others that you're a committed bisexual. It was only a half-lie, anyway. You *would* have a threesome. You just haven't had it put in front of you. Until, that is, you met Sexy Motherfucker. One or two years later, when you're in a more settled relationship, you'll probably look back and think, "Holy cats, I can't believe I did that!" It's not regret, more like it seems like it happened to another person. But it happened to you, lucky girl. Hope you are keeping scrapbook.

YOU WILL HAVE A HARD TIME GIVING UP THE PIPE

As in, the flesh pipe. The old pink hammer. The tube steak smothered in underwear. It feels like you'll never find another person who intuitively understands (and delivers) exactly what you want, whether it's being slowly licked for hours and treated like a delicate lotus flower or turned around and rammed until your teeth click. Remember the alcoholic's motto of "progress, not perfection" and try your best to remain hopeful. Sex isn't everything. (Possibly.)

MONOGAMY IS LIKE NERD DICE: MULTISIDED

Will you finally know where you stand on it? No, probably not. But if you're someone who's always said, "*Hmmm*, I don't know," when people are discussing the idea, you will probably have a little more to share on the subject. Sexy Motherfucker is anti-monogamy and believes he can quash jealousy and hundreds of years of societal directives that have been drilled into our heads simply by shaking that shimmering mane of his and saying a more enlightened, less Casanova-like version of "Hey, ladies, there's more than enough of this to go around . . ." In theory, it's tempting to believe. In practice, it's difficult.

★ ★ ★ Reviews

What Critics Are Saying About Sexy Motherfucker

"He was always up for it no matter what. No matter how much alcohol or drugs he'd had, he was simply always horny."

—MELISSA

"He unbuttoned his shirts down to his waist. He had long, curly woman hair. He looked like a young Fabio."

—TONYA

"He had a curved penis and could go and go and go."

—ELAINE

YOUR MINI PRESS KIT

Sexy Motherfucker is the guy who . . .

- ✦ Had rounded all the sexual bases and was inventing new ways to play the game by the time he got to middle school.

- ✦ Is disliked by your father and liked perhaps a little too much by your mother and sister.

- ✦ Leaves you because you're not experimental enough in bed but winds up marrying a Baptist virgin.

- ✦ Has such strong animal magnetism that even the straightest of straight guys entertains the thought of doing him.

- ✦ Practices unsafe intimacy but never unsafe intercourse.

MANNISH

BOY 4

Fig. 4a: Mannish Boy

THE MEET & GREET

Who He Is

Mannish Boy is the guy who refuses to grow up and makes all his life decisions (or, rather, indecisions) according to that goal. He goes to see every Judd Apatow movie the day it opens, laughing at the characters, not getting that he's essentially watching a big-screen depiction of his personality flaws. A comedic genius with no self-awareness. Your fifth-grade boyfriend, with the same hair and a slightly higher income.

What He's All About

A Mannish Boy is anyone who has big ideas and ambitions but remains emotionally, financially, and socially in a state of inertia. Rather than pulling himself up by his Wii straps, Mannish Boy looks to you to encourage him while simultaneously blaming you for his lack of progress. While it's true that a little immaturity is charming, you never thought you'd be the girl whose boyfriend crapped in the host's cat's litterbox as a party stunt. Despite his boyish quirks, Mannish Boy's natural charisma is a crowd-pleaser. He fits in with all kinds of friends, is adored by your parents, and is an always available weed source. Mannish Boy is also *familiar*. He's the sweet, bumbling Fozzie Bear you crushed on before you realized that no one marries Fozzie. People settle down with Kermit after brief dalliances with Animal and Gonzo.

> **PERSONAL MOTTO**
>
> *Adult supervision required.*

Turn-ons

Fresh tube socks, food in pocket form, sampler platters, formalized ridiculousness, Sarah Silverman, extended cohabitation, defending Kevin Smith as a director, faux homosexuality, inside jokes.

Turnoffs

Skinny jeans, your male best friend, Kathy Griffin, Tilda Swinton, that dipshit from The Strokes, people who are successful in their chosen occupation, sincere emotional discourse, last call.

THE HEADLINERS

Mannish Boys are rampant in the rock 'n' roll kingdom. After all, if a wildly shortsighted and unrealistic occupational choice has gotten you where you are, what reason do you have to stop now?

Here's a glam-rock Peter Pan who's been ruining TV for the better part of a decade, a trio of hip-hop icons who built a skateboarding ramp in their office, and a rap pioneer who belongs in a playpen while he's being fed cognac from a baby bottle.

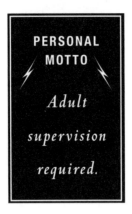

Every Rose Has Its Thorn

happy hour than you do, even though it's his first week and you've been working there forever.

STUPID ONLINE MEMES, VIDEOS, OR DEBATES

Mannish Boy is the reason for the Internet's success or its downfall, depending on whether you get your news from *The Wall Street Journal* or Fark. One thing is for sure, Mannish Boy is the dream audience for anyone trying to promote a company, product, or person off a viral video. If there's an opportunity to upload a picture and transform yourself into a lolcat or a penis face, Mannish Boy is *so down*. As you make your online rounds (don't pretend you're too good for this, we know you), look for the person being the most pithy and clever. Watch for spelling and beware of too much leetspeak. We don't want you accidentally cruising a thirteen-year-old.

His Act

aka Ways of Working the Crowd . . .

BEING "THAT GUY"

That guy is the guy who doesn't give a fuuuuuck. He's making a complete spectacle of himself, and he's probably not even under the influence of any substance. He's the person covered head to toe in body paint at an exhibition football match, the loudest at Tuesday happy hour karaoke. Ice skating in the nude? Party-crashing with Harvey Keitel? He's done it. Mannish Boy gets into epic adventures and impossible situations. He's the reason YouTube is so interesting (or, if you're a half-empty kind of person, full of total morons). If you find outlandishness attractive and are looking for a gent with an immunity to public embarrassment that rivals yours, Mannish Boy is a lock.

THIRD-WHEELING IT

Mannish Boy doesn't get into a lot of relationships. Perhaps that's why he's never cognizant of the fact that he doesn't have a date and everyone else around him does. Look for the guy chatting up the happy couple as they pick out wedding registry gifts ("No, Mike, we're not going to register for a stair lift. I don't care how convenient it'd be when we're wasted. We don't have room for it in the apartment"). Truth be told, most couples don't mind him. He's entertaining and, after years together, comic relief from the strain of day-to-day togetherness. Pay attention the next time you see a female-male-male combo. It may take a moment to figure out who's with whom (especially if the two guys in the guy-guy-girl couple wind up being gay), but often you'll be rewarded with a cute Mannish Boy for your struggle.

ENGAGING IN SOME COMPETITION THAT DOESN'T MATTER

Mannish Boys love games, whether it's Connect Four, Ultimate Frisbee, or pickup basketball. Even the ones who are athletically challenged are willing to make an exception once a fad hits the zeitgeist: dodgeball, kickball, basically anything that was popular before simulated indoor athletics came into vogue. He may own a scooter, a Vespa, a pogo stick, or, of course, a skateboard. He loves girls who can play sports. We're talking automatic dream girl privileges. When choosing between a batshit crazy girl who's been institutionalized but who kicks ass at darts and a girl who stays on top of her bills but sucks butt at soccer, Mannish Boy will take the former. Interests over character.

His Wardrobe

aka Proper & Improper Attire . . .

Fig 4b: Wacky boxers are the reverse female Viagra.

FOUR OFF THE FLOOR

It's the same four components, all put together in slight variations, like the menu at Taco Bell. Getting dressed involves grabbing several items and hoping he ends up with at least one top and one bottom. He has a set of standards, and the rest of what he owns looks like (and actually is) outfits his mother picked out for him.

What He Wears

- Jeans, baggy in the ass but otherwise somewhat attractive and current
- Sneakers or a sneaker–dress shoe hybrid. (How did these get to be a good idea? Who said it was okay for twentysomething males to walk around in souped-up Hush Puppies?)
- T-shirts he should have thrown out years ago
- T-shirts he bought as a joke
- T-shirts he got for free
- T-shirts that were stolen
- Wacky boxer shorts

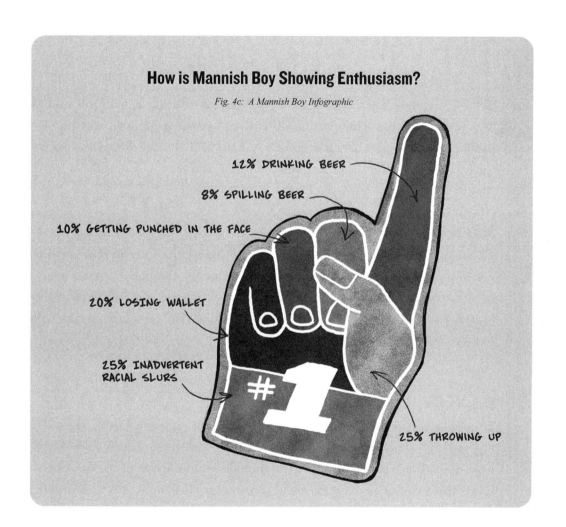

How to Get Backstage

or at the Very Least His Phone Number...

Fig. 4d: Perhaps it's time to wean him.

ACTIVELY AVOID HIM

Want to attract a Mannish Boy? Date one, or have just broken up with one (or hell, a whole string of 'em) and swear to all who will listen that you'll never date another. It's especially helpful if the breakup was bad or involved the removal of friends, possessions, or tattoos.

Why It Works

The answer reads like a butchered Rolling Stones lyric: You can always get what you don't want. You always have more than enough of what you don't need and not enough of what you do. In other words, all lids but no Tupperware. Alanis Morrisette singing songs about rain and wedding days on a community college radio station that no one will ever listen to.

BE VERY, VERY THIRSTY

Drink like the wind. Drink like a recovering sober person. Drink beers. Drink liquor. Drink shots. Yes, we know drinking's not for everyone. Yes, some Mannish Boys don't drink. However, that's not included in the scope of the book because that subset comprises such a small percentage of people. We've also left out dating tips for foreign ambassadors, vampires, and people who don't enjoy more than one lobster tail per sitting. Is that okay, Your Highness? You want inclusive, go read something from Oprah's Book Club.

 Every Rose Has Its Thorn

Why It Works

Mannish Boy loves the cocktails. He loves booze-centric events, where he'll be out longer and later and drunker than all of his compadres. For him, drinking is a prequalifier, a way to show a girl's worth her mettle. (P.S. What's a mettle?) It's lame that you have to drink to impress someone, but you've done lamer things in the interest of getting laid, like pretending you like Phish, or reading that *Ulysses* shit by James "No Fun" Joyce.

THROW HIM A SOFTBALL

The one sports metaphor with a practical application. Tell his friend you like him. Wear a quietly skanky top (no text over the tits; he'll fuck up and read it and feel too embarrassed to talk to you). A Slayer logo or something stereotypically male-oriented should do quite well. Walk up to the bar and order a hairy-chested kind of draft. Say something about an obscure post-punk band everyone thinks no one knows.

Why It Works

Mannish Boys are shy, lazy, or shy and lazy. They will not approach you unless given explicit permission. It's like when someone sends you an e-mail with the subject line *Most Life-Changing Video Ever* and you really want to see it but you can't be bothered to cut and paste the link and so you hit the delete button and move on. Mannish Boys are rarely up-and-at-'em about meeting people. Which is probably good, because on the occasions they are, they're drunk off their ass and their normally sweet-natured behavior is so out of hand they cock-block themselves.

→ PLAYLIST

Cock Rock: Songs About Male Genitalia Loved by Mannish Boys the World Over

1. **"Big Balls"—AC/DC, 1976, Albert**
   Funny from the age of thirteen up until Mannish Boy got his first testicular exam. Then not.
2. **"The Stroke"—Billy Squier, 1981, Capitol**
   What's better than a rousing stadium anthem? A rousing stadium anthem about *handjobs.*
3. **"Big Ten Inch Record"—Aerosmith, 1975, Columbia/Sony BMG**
   Lip span is about the only thing that's ten inches on Steven Tyler but Mannish Boy loves both talking about wangs and showing off his knowledge of the deep cuts.
4. **"Pearl Necklace"—ZZ Top, 1981, Warner Brothers**
   A charming number from three dudes so creepy you wouldn't accept *real* jewelry from them, let alone a gift of bodily fluid.
5. **"The Lemon Song"—Led Zeppelin, 1969, Atlantic**
   Squeeze my tasteless metaphor until the juice runs down my scrawny leather-pants-clad leg.

POP QUIZ

Mannish Boy Checklist

Determine whether your Mannish Boy is more boy than man or more man than boy with this handy list of yes/no psychosocial development indicators.

1. Does he have a checking account?   Yes [ ]   No [ ]
2. Beer paraphernalia as part of household décor?   Yes [ ]   No [ ]
3. Has he played paintball more than once in the past twelve months?   Yes [ ]   No [ ]
4. Maintain a crush on Jessica Biel, Simpson, or Alba?   Yes [ ]   No [ ]
5. Spend the majority of after-work hours in front of a TV or video game apparatus?   Yes [ ]   No [ ]
6. Does he have a really great idea for a T-shirt company?   Yes [ ]   No [ ]
7. What about a start-up?   Yes [ ]   No [ ]
8. Could he easily see himself going gay for Andy Samberg?   Yes [ ]   No [ ]
9. Does he get faux flirty with male friends when wasted?   Yes [ ]   No [ ]
10. Does he think it's the most hilarious thing ever?   Yes [ ]   No [ ]
11. Did he go see *Knocked Up* and argue with you coming out of the theater?   Yes [ ]   No [ ]

SCORING

MOSTLY YES = MANNISH BOY

Grown-up but not ready to grow up. Good during a rebound or other type of transition. A guy with the potential to have no potential. Full-on acceptance of his limited capacities or immediate exploration of other options is encouraged.

MOSTLY NO = BOYISH MAN

He's no wise elder, but he's working on it. Ideal for upwardly mobile college grads or for party girls who want to hang up their halter tops. An excellent match for those looking to improve their ready-to-assemble furniture collection and/or appease pushy wannabe-grandparents.

IF YOU DECIDE TO BOOK HIM FOR ONE NIGHT ONLY

aka the Ins and Outs of Being Friends with Benefits...

 *The Pros*

HE'S GOOD TO GO

Unlike other guys who need to be in the mood or bare minimum physically present, Mannish Boy is always in the mood. His responsibilities are few and his schedule is structured so that leisure time is plentiful and available. The only exception would be when he's exceptionally inebriated. Then you'll have to go to his place and take a gamble: He might be up for it, or he might be passed out in front of the TV or on top of his gaming console.

HE'S GOOD FOR GETTING ACTUAL SLEEP

Mannish Boy isn't big on postcoital formalities, which for a fuck buddy is an excellent quality to have. Some guys will chat your ear off, others will try to attack you for a Round 2. Mannish Boy will give you a nice smooch and a "Good job!" butt pat and then make his way to the other side of the bed. Or town. Whichever you prefer. Just imagine being able to have great sex and then get to sleep and have your space. You want a summer hookup? Put Mannish Boy at the top of your list. There's no sticky, sweaty clinging—perfect for July and August.

HE'S EASY TO PLEASE

He responds well to the basics. You won't be administering a handjob until your hand falls off or giving a BJ until your jaw needs rewiring. Mannish Boy won't teach you anything new, but he won't sketch you out, either. He knows a couple of different positions and does them well. It's like the favorite restaurant you always go to and always order the same thing, but it happens to be penis instead of stir-fry.

The Cons

HE'S A MOMENT ASSASSIN

Ever had a guy look you between the thighs and start humming the theme from *Jaws*? What about give you a wedgie or put a temporary Hannah Montana tattoo on his testicles? There's a time to joke and a time to be serious. Mannish Boy does not seem to have grasped this concept. He'll give you zerberts on your privates, while doing Obama impressions as he's pumping away behind you. Funny men are great, but mad props to anyone who can deal with that and still orgasm.

HE'S NOT PREPARED FOR CLASS

He never has condoms. His bed never has sheets. You get up for a glass of water after doing the deed and are forced to stand at the sink refilling a shot glass. He's not a jerk. He just doesn't think of these things. Problem is, he's just a sex partner, so it's not like you can nag. (Not that it would make a difference. Even if he were your boyfriend, he wouldn't exactly be following you around with a Swiffer.)

HIS FOREPLAY SUCKS

Not everyone needs Portishead and scented candles, and there are some guys who can get away with an abbreviated warm-up. Mannish Boy is not one of them. He'll make The Triangle (boob, boob, vadge) and then hit the runway for takeoff. It's serviceable, but soooooooooooo predictable. On the days you need a little extra it's very annoying. Painful, even. You don't go up to a girl and smash and grab. You lovingly admire the jewels before asking them to be brought out of the case.

 Every Rose Has Its Thorn

IF YOU DECIDE TO MAKE HIM THE HOUSE BAND

aka from Groupie to Girlfriend and Beyond . . .

 *The Pros*

HE ACCEPTS YOU

He doesn't have a problem with your computer screen being dirty, the books you read, or the friends you go out with on the weekend. He's not slipping you adult education catalogues or gym brochures. According to him, there's no better you than the person you are right now, which is a huge relief to those of us with scathing inner critics. In fact, if he had it his way, everyone would never change—most of all himself.

HE WON'T PUSH YOU OUT OF THE NEST

The exact opposite is what's on his agenda. He isn't thinking about moving in or grad school or ends of leases or how your pets are meshing. He doesn't lose sleep wondering whether it's a problem that you're having sex less than you were when you first met each other. Mannish Boy lives his life in periods of twenty-four hours. Which leaves you free to focus on everything else you've got going on in your life other than your relationship. Women are always characterized as being the ultimate communicators, but we're avoidant, too, and it's nice to have this escape valve.

HE'S A HUMAN RUBBER CHICKEN
Mannish Boy always has something ridiculous and perfect to say. It's the kind of funny you'll be searching for in all the rest of your relationships if you break up. Years from now, you'll be walking down the street, and something random will happen. You want to call him and tell him about it so bad your funny bone literally aches. Fuck Lord Byron. Fuck Lloyd Dobler with his boom box. Fuck Johnny Depp and his catfish mustache and pretty-boy eyeliner. Humor is the most important trait in a boyfriend, and one of the most irreplaceable, too.

YOU WON'T REALLY GET TO KNOW HIM
It's not Mannish Boy being cool or mysterious, it's him being weird and closed off and not knowing how to deal with women. It's being depressed and refusing to see a shrink. It's not about men being men; it's about you knowing more about his guacamole preferences than his personal morals. Everything's this big vacuum. What's the point? You ask yourself this frequently. If I'm going to stay in a country and tour the same areas everyone else gets to see again and again,

why am I paying such a high day rate? It'd be more fun to go slutting through Europe.

HE'S UPTIGHT BUT THINKS HE'S "LAID-BACK"

As long as you let him do what he wants to do and make the relationship happy and comfortable, Mannish Boy will have no problem. Watch out, though; he'll get pissed the minute you start making waves. You do the work, but you will not get thanked for it. You will bring up the elephant in the room but be chided for seeing it. You will argue; he'll give a little. You promise to do the same. You come through; he doesn't. Repeat the same pattern all over and it's the classic no-win situation.

HE'S NOT SELF-AWARE

He's almost self-aware, which is too bad. If he were completely out of touch with his emotions it'd be much easier to get rid of him. He fake Hammer-dances on the edge of emotional awareness, and that makes it even more devastating. You can see that hint of grown-up poking through, the light at the end of the adolescence. Mannish Boy is about as aware as you were when you were fifteen, which is to say you were getting there but still had a lot to learn. Will he learn it? Maybe. Will you be around?

HOW TO END IT HARMONIOUSLY

WITH A "DARE TO BE GREAT AND THEN FAIL" MOMENT

In every relationship there will be a set of circumstances in which women are made and men are born. In this type of crisis, you will respond, and Mannish Boy will continue to act hapless, helpless, and sullen. You can force that occasion (more on that in a bit), or you can let the universe do its thing and wait for your car to break down, a relative to die, or a persnickety landlord to throw you out of your apartment. Then, in what twelve-steppers call "a moment of clarity," it will all become apparent. It will be "go time," and you'll be gone. Out of there. You will miss Mannish Boy but you won't. Ironically, you will probably embark on a period in which you act profoundly immature. Jägerbombs for everyone! See you at Forever 21.

WITH A HOBBY

Hey, you. Yes, you, the perfect one. You spend so much time thinking about Mannish Boy's failings and how you can fix them that you barely know who you are anymore. What did you do before you spent all that time resenting and glowering? Get something to do. Occupy yourself. When you do, two things will happen: (1) You'll feel better about yourself, and (2) the differences between you and Mannish Boy will be thrown into even sharper relief. You'll finally get the self-confidence and distance you need to leave this lovable sack of suck.

WITH A PIGGYBACK ON SOMETHING ELSE
Attach the dump to something good, whether it's his finally getting a job or his friend moving to town or his promotion to assistant manager at the sub shop. Alternately, attach the dump to something bad: Mannish Boy fighting with his best friend, his engine block blowing up. Mannish Boy is big on the universe being out to get him and loves nothing more than a tangible confirmation (bonus points if he can talk about it on Facebook). You'll be written off as one of the haters and be able to escape with minimal hassle, kind of like how political scandals always seem to accidentally coincide with big sports wins or the demise of a young, attractive starlet.

HOW TO KEEP MAKING SWEET MUSIC TOGETHER

TAKE A BREAKOUT ROLE
Many women in a long-term relationship with Mannish Boy complain that they always have to play the bad cop. The heavy. The weird part here is that a lot of them bring it upon themselves. Mannish Boy isn't judging you while you race

around and clean up the house party. He's too busy doing beer bongs with your guests to notice. He's also not worrying about whether you'll have the best Halloween couples costume. You're the one who spent all night sewing miniature leaves onto your matching trees-who-look-like-Christopher-Walken outfits. He would have been just as happy donning a pair of cardboard boxes, breaking out the old Sharpie, and writing MR. AND MRS. ROBOT on them. Try slacking off and watch how the world doesn't fall apart. Fewer arguments and more good times are sure to follow.

REMEMBER WHO OWNS WHAT

His life is his. Your life is yours. "Uh-uh. Not if you're in it for the long haul." Okay, fine then. Ninety percent of his life is his, and 90 percent of your life is yours. The sentiment still stands, though. There's little you can do if you're unhappy with his creative inertia or his unwillingness to try harder at his job. There are quite a few women who live happily with their Mannish Boys, dealing with the bad (irresponsibility, stubbornness, etc.) in order to get at the good (sweetness, down-to-earthness, devotion). There're also quite a few Mannish Boys who morph into something more resembling an adult over time. However, this is rare, and if you want to succeed with a Mannish Boy, you've got to accept the goods as is and be willing to accept that nothing may ever change and that, even if it does, it won't be for a long, long while.

THE HAND THAT ROCKS THE CRADLE ALSO DECIDES WHAT'S FOR DINNER

Being with a Mannish Boy means being in charge of decisions both big and small. It also means putting up with a fair bit of indecisiveness, as Mannish Boy is just as uncomfortable selecting and purchasing a car as a brand of orange juice. After a long week of taking everyone's bullshit, the thought of having to come up with Saturday and Sunday's social plans is enough to drive you to murder. But put down that apple corer and look at it this way: At least you're getting to do all the stuff you want to do. Mannish Boy has tastes similar to yours and he'll rarely give you an argument. If he does, you can simply say, "Okay, then, let's hear your plan," and you'll find him quickly backing down. Should you leave Mannish Boy and enter into a new relationship with a more decisive type, you may be dismayed to find that your compromise muscles have atrophied to the point that they don't work anymore.

FOR THE RECORD

aka Relationship Lessons from the School of Rock . . .

KNOW WHEN YOU ARE HERE AND THEY ARE THERE

You haven't wanted to believe it, because you're stubborn and loyal and you bought all that West Elm stuff not too long ago. The living room is *finally* in a good place, and you really, really wanted this to work out. Can an adult and a non-adult make it work? It depends. Are you willing to relax a little? Not take on more than you have to? Look at it this way: You can't get paid for it, thanked for it, or even recognized for it. So why do it at all? That's not to say Mannish Boy is free from responsibility. Just as you have to chill with the ten-year plan, he has to step up his game a bit and get closer to the realm of real live adult.

AVAILABILITY AIN'T SO ATTRACTIVE

Mannish Boy was great when you first met. When asked, "What do you want to do?" he always answered something like "I don't care, I just want to be with you," and you thought you had hit the jackpot. It was only later that you found out those words were Mannish Boy for: (1) I don't have any ideas; (2) I don't want to be responsible for coming up with any ideas; and (3) Even if I *did* have an idea, I don't have any money to spend on it. Yes, he can be with you as often as you want, and for some of you codependent types it's a dream come true. *You mean I have someone to go buy microwave popcorn and paper towels with?*

BEING A GROWN-UP SUCKS SOMETIMES

Case in point: Breaking up with a Mannish Boy. Who knew he'd be so hard to get over? You want to hear his disgruntled pigeon impression one more time and cry when you discover you've accidentally deleted it from your voicemail. As you venture back out into the dating world, you're still going to find yourself drawn to these types. Could it be that you don't want to grow up yourself? You like being the beleaguered girlfriend? You like feeling needed? It's something to think about as you're scrubbing the last traces of Mannish Boy out of your shower grout.

Every Rose Has Its Thorn

★★★ Reviews

What Critics Are Saying About Mannish Boy

"He's every dude I ever dated. Which is part of the reason why I never date anymore."

—Lori

"'L' was this boyfriend that I had for almost three years. I paid his rent for two years because he was working on a novel and he could not be bothered with getting a job. I got sucked into it. I'm suing him now."

—Jan

"It had been a really decent night. Dinner and TV. We ended up having sex. Ten minutes into it, I take off my shirt. He takes off his shirt. We're going at it. He looks at me and goes, 'Oh wow. Fat people sex.' I immediately stopped and was like, 'What did you just call me?' He immediately backed up and said, 'No, I meant me! I meant me!' He was always being inappropriate."

—Maria

YOUR MINI PRESS KIT

Mannish Boy is the guy who . . .

- Owns a gorilla suit, but not an interview suit.

- Doesn't work on his grad school apps, because he "doesn't have the time," but spends upward of two hours a day in useless flame wars on 4chan.

- Takes you to an ironic restaurant for your anniversary.

- Calls you by your last name . . . in bed.

- Uses a broomstick as a curtain rod and a T-shirt as a pillowcase yet spends entire paychecks optimizing the gaming capabilities of his computer.

- Wants sex but not as much as he wants to watch *Adult Swim*.

PART-TIME

LOVER

Fig. 5a: Part Time Lover

THE MEET & GREET

Who He Is

Part-Time Lover is any guy you've dated who's only halfway in the relationship, if you could even call it that. What do you call someone who started out as a childhood crush, worked his way up to boyfriend, moved cross-country, broke up with you and decided he was gay, got back together with you in the context of an "open relationship," cheated on you, got dumped by you, then showed up on your doorstep to propose marriage, only to bang a random a week later. Now you see him only occasionally, ostensibly for sex, but he has erection issues, so usually it turns into a combination of cuddling and bickering.

Sorry, didn't mean to dump all that on you. You don't deserve that. It's way too early in the chapter. Let's start over.

Part-Time Lover is the known and unknown. The push. The pull. What you want but don't want. What you have but don't have. He's unpredictable, and often it drives you to do things you later regret and behave like a hot mess. You don't know where you stand, yet you don't want to ask because you're afraid of the answer. You want off the roller coaster because it's making you ill, but the operator looks like a young Hugh Jackman, shirtless.

Starting to get the picture?

What He's All About

Now, unlike the other types described in this book, Part-Time Lover enjoys a rich diversity.

In no particular order (except, uh, numeric), here are the ten most common variations of this species:

1. THE ALREADY HAS SOMEONE

He's married, girlfriended, obsessed with an ex, or otherwise not available. We feel sorry for you, but in the same way we do for people who purchase tickets to anything with "Part III" in the title. You knew what you were in for from the beginning.

2. THE DISTANT AND IN DENIAL

All contact comes from you. If you didn't reach out, you're not sure you'd ever hear from him again. You call him on it, and he acts absentminded or gently implies that you're being needy. Are you? Your memory of what he looks like is fading, but he's so good with the counterarguments that you start to doubt yourself.

3. THE DISTANT AND PROUD OF IT

"I don't need you, so please don't need me!" is the constantly reinforced message. He's always warning you not to get your hopes up. He won't commit, and you accept that. You really do. But you don't see the harm in meeting for coffee with separate checks. It's only been sixteen months of e-mailing. Next time you won't be so forward.

4. THE ACTUALLY DISTANT
He lives somewhere geographically inconvenient. Though you try to keep the relationship going with calls and chats and texts, and even went so far as to get over your fear of webcams. He won't move. You won't move. Stalemate.

5. THE ZOMBIE
This is the ex that you can't get rid of, whether he's part of a vicious cycle of F/F/F/F (fight, fuck, fight, fuck) or an ex so sweet and lovelorn that he sends birthday e-cards to your mother, sister, and current boyfriend.

6. THE HOT/COLD
Oh, darling. We feel for you. This one's brutal. This is the Part-Time Lover who will be all up in your face one week and then totally absent the next. How can you go from calling someone pet names and planning vacations with her to dropping the bomb that you're still seeing other people? This is a guy who treats you like a fern, bringing you to the brink with neglect and then flooding you with nourishing affection to make you feel alive again. Then the cycle repeats itself until he finally tosses you out.

7. THE "1,000 PERCENT BUSY"
We'd tell you more about this one, but we don't have the bandwidth. Sorry. Can you meet next week? No, wait. We'll be out that week. What about the week after the week after? No, wait. Oh, well. We'll get back to you. When? We don't know. We'll tell you when it's a little less hectic.

8. THE RUNNER

He bolts when he's sad. He bolts when he's happy. He bolts when there's no good reason, other than he likes the drama of making up and breaking up and it's been two whole days without a fight and now he's feeling a little antsy. He's going to a shrink to figure out why he does this, but so far he's walked out on the first couple of visits . . .

9. THE EVERYTHING BUT

He's not your "boyfriend," but you've been together ten years. He lives with you, splits the bills, participates in household chores, and knows you like the kitty litter in the green box, not the blue box, because of that one time you used the blue it was all grody and nonclumping. Why is this Part-Time Lover so afraid of taking it further? We don't know. He just is. With all the disposable marriages out there, it's not always the worst plan of action.

10. THE WTHJH

This is the guy you've been on several dates with. It seems to be going well. Then—What the Hell Just Happened? You never hear from him again. On the off, off (OFF) chance he was cool enough to leave a text message, it's something to the effect of "I can't do this," and reads like a ransom note. You're baffled. Your friends have had the last three brunches ruined with a blow-by-blow dissection of the story. Look, there was no way you could have seen this coming. Some daters just act like weirdos.

A PARTIAL LIST OF ROCK 'N' ROLL'S MOST FAMOUS PART-TIME LOVERS

Rock 'n' roll doesn't always produce the most linear of relationships. Whether it's because they're constantly flying first-class or abusing illegal substances, it's hard to stay grounded. Throw in the naked enabling of an adoring public, and you've got yourself a whole slew of celebrity couples who are constantly rewriting the boy-meets-girl story.

TOMMY & PAMMY

Mötley Crüe drummer Tommy Lee married actress/model/epic eyebrow-plucking failure Pamela Anderson in 1995 within ninety-six hours of knowing her. Since then, they've filed for divorce twice, made up twice, had some run-ins with the law, and are, as this book goes to press, either back together or officially split apart. They say all the attempts at reconciliation are for the kids, but we think it's the sex. When God puts two sets of genitals like that together, let no man tear asunder.

SONNY & CHER

The pop music duo with a serious thing for polyester hit big in the mid-'60s with hits like "I Got You Babe" and "Baby Don't Go." They met, made music, married, had a messy divorce, and then reunited for another in a series of seriously bad series. Decades passed. Sonny passed. But whether it's a karaoke duet, a couples Halloween costume, or a crossword puzzle answer, the two are forever united in the collective consciousness, here and now as well as in the hereafter.

STEVIE & LINDSEY

Two members of the British rock band that's had almost everyone as a member, they kept Fleetwood Mac going, despite an onslaught of bummers: battles with bandmates, each other, drugs, the press, and producers. We doubt this living example of "Don't shit where you eat" has stopped anyone from pursuing a workplace romance. The clothes were too cool, the fame too big, not to mention all the awesome songs that came out of it.

GWEN & GAVIN

They met in the mid-'90s when both of their bands were at the height of their fame (Gwen: No Doubt; Gavin: Bush), Clinton was in office, and a grown woman leaving the house in a baby-tee and sparkly dragonfly barrettes was considered appropriate. They kept up a long-distance relationship for over half a decade before getting married in 2002. There were rocky periods. How cool would *you* be if your new husband's ex turned up with a teenage daughter? Oh yeah, and she's a model. Gwen and Gavin made it through, producing a couple of ridiculously adorable and better-dressed-than-you'll-ever-be offspring in the process. Proof that time and distance can harm some relationships but also make others more solid.

His Regular Venues, His Act, His Wardrobe, etc., etc.

We know this section looks empty, way empty. Even emptier than all the others. That's because Part-Time Lover keeps dodging us. How are we supposed to give you the low-down on how he walks, talks, acts, etc., if he won't return our calls?

Use this space to sketch an image of what he was like the last time you saw him. Then kiss it and tuck it under your pillow along with some sort of talisman or charm: a small piece of cube steak, perhaps; some velvet ribbon; a massaging gel insole.

Perhaps you'll have better luck getting him to show up than we will.

Part-Time Lover

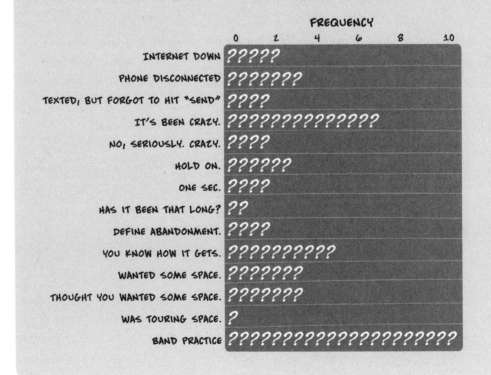

Every Rose Has Its Thorn

★★★ Reviews

What Critics Are Saying About Part-Time Lover

"We both had someone. It was at summer camp. I was a counselor. We would meet every third day on the lacrosse field and make out."

—Jessica

"He was a bipolar mess. I would see him every now and then. When he was up and positive and happy it was the most amazing thing, and that's when I would see him. Then he would get depressed and I wouldn't see him at all. One day, his female roommate said to me, 'Which one are you? Are you the really religious one?' I said, 'No, I'm not. I didn't know there were others.' The same girl and I later ended up getting topless and making out."

—Emily

"I woke up in the middle of the night and he was gone. Eventually I found a note scrawled on a coffee filter that said, 'You were dreaming, I had insomnia. I'll call you.' And then I called him crying and saying, 'I feel so trashy.' He was nonchalant. We didn't see each other for three weeks. Then he invited me to Thanksgiving. Anyway, we have two kids and live together now."

—Angie

YOUR MINI PRESS KIT

Part-Time Lover is the guy who . . .

- Takes all his possessions with him when he leaves your place, even though you live together.

- You acquire new information and updates about through people you've just met.

- You've broken up with so many times you no longer bother updating friends, family, or Facebook.

- Goes through relationship-questioning periods and freakouts so regularly you and your shrink have been able to make anticipatory adjustments in your medication.

- Is "too busy" for a blowjob.

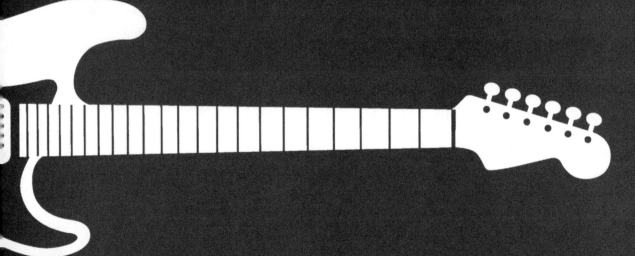

STUFF

THE MEET & GREET

Who He Is

Most Likely to Succeed or—more likely—Most Likely to *Pretend* to Have Succeeded by Going to Your High School Reunion and Writing "Consulting" Next to "Occupation" Instead of Admitting That He's the Night Manager of a Quizno's Franchise. The poster boy for hubris. A guy with all the makings of a sweetheart, if only he could stop giving a shit about making people think he's King Shit and just let go.

What He's All About

Whether he's got thousands in the bank or Rent-A-Center furniture under threat of repossession, Mr. Big Stuff's burning mission is to convince everyone around him—especially you—that he's extremely important. He doesn't have time for this. He's on a call. He'll have his people call your people. Ciao! He has to go. For all the fakery, he does have the human capital: connections, peeps, hookups, guys he knows. He'll go broke trying to impress you, which can be intoxicating, especially if you're used to the kind of dates where you order cheese fries and go Dutch. His insecurity makes you feel powerful. You want to get at what's behind it. A well-placed high school humiliation anecdote here, a Budweiser-and-corndog beach picnic there, and somehow you become convinced he's a nice guy who just happens to get a little anal about his wine order.

Mr. Big Stuff

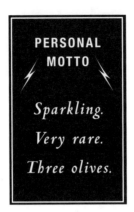

PERSONAL MOTTO

Sparkling.
Very rare.
Three olives.

Turn-ons

Designer brands, networking, '80s Night, chatting up restroom attendants, working hard, playing harder, passing Breathalyzers, speaking glowingly of his mother, heavy watches, valet parking, quoting great literature.

Turnoffs

Secondhand stores, pictures of himself from seventh grade, weak cellular reception, every song by The Cure except "Just Like Heaven," those careless guys down at the car wash, unreturned texts, Michael Cera, reading great literature.

THE HEADLINERS

Mr. Big Stuff is one of the most common rocker archetypes. If a male musician's not one, chances are he has been through a phase where he was one, and is now on a path toward spiritual enlightenment.

As an introduction, here's a hip-hop artist who's made his vanity an international brand, a washed-up pop star still partying like it's 1995, and a singer-songwriter whose last marriage included a daughter/maid of honor four years younger than his bride.

 Every Rose Has Its Thorn

KANYE WEST

Who He Is
Rapper, producer, indie hipster sycophant; caps-lock happy blogger; unrepentant designer bag and shoe whore; Taylor Swift dream crusher.

What Makes Him Such a Mr. Big Stuff
Takes every opportunity to announce his greatness, no matter how offensive or inappropriate; speaks about his postdeath legacy in a way that makes you want to help it get there sooner; has his manicured little paw in everything but a sincere commitment to nothing.

"I have liked big t*ts ever since I was a kid. I was breastfed for too long I think. It messed me up."

Kanye West,
New York,
April 2008

Mr. Big Stuff Highlights
- A self-confessed sex addict who can trace his start all the way back to the seventh grade, when he made a computer game featuring anthropomorphic penises battling ghost vaginas.
- Wrote a song decrying gold diggers but drapes every square inch of skin in Louis Vuitton and Rolexes like so much rich-guy chum.
- With his shutter shades, argyle prints, V-necks, and highwaters, he is largely responsible for the terrifying trend of douchebag in nerd's clothing.

Mr. Big Stuff 143

MARK McGRATH

"I'm not romantic in that Hallmark way."

Mark McGrath,
People,
November 16, 1998

Who He Is
Lead singer of Sugar Ray, a late-'90s several-hit wonder best known for songs you feel dirty about singing along to on the radio; TV personality; Clairol Frost & Tip spokesman; pussy machine of the county-fair circuit.

What Makes Him Such a Mr. Big Stuff
Voted "Sexiest Rocker" of 1998 by *People* magazine. Time has marched on; his ego has not. Bolsters his career by hanging with low-self-esteem people more attractive than himself, i.e., *Extra* cohosts and Pussycat Dolls.

Mr. Big Stuff Highlights
- Is so into status symbols that he has a Rolex and a Cadillac tattooed on his body, right next to a large set of praying hands. For baby Jesus.
- Recorded and released an album called *Music for Cougars*. According to our calculations, McGrath is forty+ years old. Age denial much?
- Has been with girlfriend for fifteen years and is just now starting to talk about marriage. Why? Because having a dog has "matured him."

 Every Rose Has Its Thorn

BILLY JOEL

Who He Is
Christie Brinkley's ex-husband, patron saint of short guys, The "Piano" and "DUI Arrest" Man. Definitely *not* the one who started the fire. Part of an elite group of individuals who tried to kill themselves by ingesting furniture polish.

What Makes Him Such a Mr. Big Stuff
Prefers the company of females decades younger and/or models. Puts on working-class airs while pulling in Oprah money. Known for indoor sunglasses and sharkskin jackets—classy time!

> *"I had no idea that she was that young."*
>
> Billy Joel talking about ex-wife Katie Lee in *Details*, July 2008

Mr. Big Stuff Highlights
- Down with his New York roots, but not so down that he doesn't charge rent-poor New Yorkers one bazillion dollars for seats at his concerts.
- According to the RIAA, the sixth-bestselling recording artist in the United States and still making music. Looks like *someone* doesn't know how to put down the microphone and give the other kids a turn.
- 95.38 percent of all unbearable karaoke performances by irritating and overpaid bosses include at least one song from his oeuvre.

Mr. Big Stuff

His Regular Venues

aka Where You'll Find Him . . .

THE DRY CLEANERS

Mr. Big Stuff loves the idea of someone besides himself or his mother taking care of his pit-stained Oxfords and wine-stained French cuffs. There's something about walking out of a storefront with an armful of hangers that gives him an extra spring in his step, an extra confidence that puts him in the mood to approach and be approachable. For here is a man who owns shirts. Shirts with rich fabrics and buttons. Shirts other than the one he happens to be wearing right now. He has no time for Tide or spray starch. He has a Lucite paperweight, one-third of a fifth of Jameson's, and a tube of athlete's foot cream in his desk drawer. Saunter in with a miniskirt and watch the action unfold.

A WINE, MARTINI, OR CIGAR BAR

Mr. Big Stuff enjoys any dimly lit establishment in which you can choose from a minimum of ten pages of items in a leather-bound folder. This gives him the opportunity to show off his knowledge and distance himself psychologically from the Natty Light–chugging frat boy he undoubtedly was several years ago. It's not getting shit-faced if it costs a lot of money and you put it on a credit card. Though he may say he comes to these male bastions because he wants a break from the meat markets and pickup joints, he's really waiting for that one girl who orders his favorite single malt. Stereotype-wise, it's akin to a woman camp-

 Every Rose Has Its Thorn

ing out at the ice cream shop waiting for Hugh Grant's twin to saunter in and order her favorite flavors in a waffle cone. In other words: Not. Gonna. Happen. However, if you're ever in a dream-fulfilling mood, you know where to go.

WHEREVER EXPENSIVE GOODS ARE SOLD

When Mr. Big Stuff has a girlfriend, he loves to whine about how much he hates shopping. Truth is, he loves it. He just has a different style, spending hours surfing for the perfect snowboard, titanium hard drive case, or outdoor grill. He's been known to "visit" favorite watches at the jeweler's. He drives to car dealerships on his lunch hour just to take test drives and fondle glossy brochures. Not a prayer. The hunt is what's important. The next time you're shopping in the tony section of town, keep your eyes peeled for the guy on the verge of an impulse purchase and provide him that little extra reinforcement. The first number he enters into that ridiculously overpriced cell phone just might be yours.

His Act

aka Ways of Working the Crowd . . .

GETTING PEOPLE'S CONTACT INFORMATION

Mr. Big Stuff was the kid who broke his arm in a heroic Pee Wee football accident and wouldn't rest until he had the entire middle school sign his cast, then cried when it was time to cut it off. Whether it's punching the info into his cell phone or scribbling it on a receipt from Banana Republic, Mr. Big Stuff will get your vitals and make an earnest promise to call. While it's easy to take this as an expression of interest, remember it's still a crapshoot. As is every other word that comes out of his mouth. Mr. Big Stuff likes having a pretty girl's phone number at his disposal more than he does the terrifying thought of actually having to call her up and ask her out.

EXPRESSING ANGER IN A SOCIALLY ACCEPTABLE MANNER

Out of all the guys with anger issues, Mr. Big Stuff has perhaps the most. Problem is, he doesn't feel free to cry or get all wired and smash up public property like Bad Company—two common male outlets. He'd rather play über-violent video games at Dave & Buster's or criticize drive-thru employees; get in flame wars in ESPN chat rooms; take pickup games at the public park way, way too seriously; or drive like a complete fucking asshole.

TALKING ABOUT HIS PASSIONS

Mr. Big Stuff loves his hobbies, of which he has a hundred. The more unlikely they are, the better, but Mr. Big Stuff tends to stay away from the low-profile (whittling, egg poaching), and opt for something more showy. Ideally, he'll be able to attach the equipment around on the back of his car or be seen about town wearing a motocross helmet or wet suit. Then he'll inwardly will all in the immediate vicinity to ask him about it so he can downplay its cool factor and appear nonplussed and humble. He's been known to throw himself into a sport and buy all the equipment, only to abandon it a few months later. Except when asked about it, he'll make it seem like his interest in aikido is still going strong. Being a Renaissance man is important to Mr. Big Stuff. He wants to be seen as something more than just another paycheck-chasing drone. Indoor rock climbing brings him closer to God, as does the smell of a new car and a 1986 Merlot.

His Wardrobe

aka Proper & Improper Attire . . .

Fig. 6b:
His designer toothbrush costs more than your paycheck.

COUNTRY CLUB CROSS-DRESSING

Mr. Big Stuff is a sartorial Jekyll and Hyde. By day, it's all-American classics: polos and khakis aka Ralph Lauren. By night, it's bad-boy rebel aka Ed Hardy: "*Rawwwr!* I'm a tiger!" It's too bad the two designers can't get it together and come out with a seersucker suit with little cobras and tattoo hearts printed all over it. Mr. Big Stuffs would spend a fortune. We digress. The point is that Mr. Big Stuff wants to dress like he owns a yacht but at any time could take off on his motorcycle.

What He Wears

We sneaked into Mr. Big Stuff's closet while he was at the auto detailer. While there, we were able to conduct a quick survey. The results are as follows:

Mr. Big Stuff

- 3 business suits, navy
- 3 business suits, black
- 1 obscenely expensive snowboarding outfit
- 36 button-down shirts, all the same cut and fabric, all from a tailor who Mr. Big Stuff believes is "like my uncle" but is actually counting the days until he never has to wait on people like Mr. Big Stuff because he makes millions from his adult website
- 1 pair of gold sneakers endorsed by his favorite hip-hop star, which he'll never have the guts to wear
- 7 pairs of dress slacks, varying sizes
- 1 to 3 sets of workout clothes, designer label. Head to toe—bandana, shirt, shorts—all with the same tasteful little logo. Because butt sweat is best absorbed by shorts that cost $95.
- 3 to 5 pieces of flair. This could include but is not limited to: a marijuana leaf necklace; an afro wig; an uncharacteristically indie or feminine accoutrement. Whatever it is, he'll be sure to make it his Facebook ID photo so everyone can see he's not just a working stiff. He's a wild card. He'll jam the printer and not take responsibility. He's done it before.

Fig. 6c: *A Mr. Big Stuff Infographic*

How to Get Backstage

or at the Very Least His Phone Number . . .

*Fig. 6d:
If there isn't a velvet rope,
Mr. Big Stuff isn't there.*

TALK SHIT

If you're at a bar and see a group of guys playing pool, talk loudly about how you could take them, even if the only billiards experience you have is swallowing the pool cue chalk when you were six (you thought it was Bubble Yum) and landing in the ER. You pooped blue for the better part of a week. Anyway, look your most attractive and then jabber on about your skill at bowling, karaoke, trivia, or darts. Be noisy. Be obnoxious. You're doing it right when your friends start rolling their eyes and Mr. Big Stuff uses his to stare holes through your blouse.

Why It Works

Mr. Big Stuff thrives on competition, but he'd never initiate a fight with a female. However, he will when it's socially safe to do so, that is, when people are hitting things with sticks or trying to get things to land on targets. This type of playful competition is irresistible to Mr. Big Stuff, who—after years of dating vapid mannequins—will find you so exotic for having an opinion you might as well have a robot arm and a prehensile vagina. He will learn later that you actually are shit-talking and argumentative . . . when he's in too far to back out. Sucker!

Every Rose Has Its Thorn

GO DO SOMETHING YOU HATE

Take salsa dancing lessons, do some speed-dating, or ride go-karts. The more out of character it is, the better. Don't worry; Mr. Big Stuff doesn't necessarily engage in this type of activity either. Mr. Big Stuff has a job or friends or friends of friends (or all three) that take him these kinds of places. He also never turns down an invite. You never know when there will be an opportunity to network or get a good deal on a time-share, vintage pinball machine, or coke-for-Ecstasy swap.

Why It Works

Did we mention girls? He's on the hunt for those as well. He sees you looking uncomfortable (read: defenseless) and wants to turn that frown upside down. He may have a girlfriend now, but don't worry. He can still get your number for later. Is that Jen with one *n* or two? Oh, wait. He has more than one Jenn S. with two *n*'s in his phone. Can he get the rest of your last name as well?

GO TO McDONALD'S OR STARBUCKS

Mr. Big Stuff is a creature of habit. Depending on the day of the week, he's hitting either Starbucks for his morning java infusion or Mickey D's to get some fat/salt/refined sugar for his hangover. If you're already patronizing these places, try going to the one down the block. Just remember to stick with it for a few weeks. You can't switch back and forth. It's like the roulette wheel. You bet black, it'll hit on red.

Why It Works

This is a place of comfort for him. If he sees you regularly in his sacred space, there will be all sorts of automatic positive associations. He will be able to impress you with his order (or disgust you if it's McDonald's) and make chitchat about the super awesome job that he's going off to that day. Do this once or twice and he'll be asking you to get coffee, which will be awkward since that's what you're already doing, but fret not, it's not coffee he's after.

 Every Rose Has Its Thorn

PLAYLIST

Lucky 7: A No-Fail Set List for Mr. Big Stuff to Get His Club On

1. **"I'm Too Sexy"—Right Said Fred, 1990, Charisma**
   Rips off shirt. *"Wheeee! I'm gay!"* (You know he's not gay, don't you?)
2. **"Hey Ya!"—Outkast, 2003, LaFace**
   Requests it every office Christmas party. Every year, the DJ "forgets" to play it until Mr. Big Stuff leaves or passes out.
3. **"Bad Boys"—Inner Circle, 1987, Ras**
   Sings along in a Jamaican accent while adding *Cool Runnings* to the Netflix queue on his iPhone.
4. **"Just a Gigolo/Ain't Got Nobody"—David Lee Roth, 1985, Warner Brothers**
   Clumsily attempts a Fred Astaire dance using a folding chair and a pretzel rod as props.
5. **"Soul Man"—The Blues Brothers, 1978, Atlantic Records**
   Tells you boring story about first time he saw the movie while toasting Belushi's untimely demise with shots.
6. **"Tubthumping"—Chumbawamba, 1997, EMI**
   A song about drinking whiskey, vodka, and lager in succession isn't indicative of alcoholism if there's a catchy beat that goes along.
7. **"Closing Time"—Semisonic, 1997, MCA**
   Makes him un-ironically misty. One in ten times it will have a side effect of getting him un-ironically laid by a wounded puppy-seeking she-drunk.

POP QUIZ

Are You a Future Mrs. Big Stuff?

Take this quiz and find out if you've always been attracted to this type or if your big ego fetish is newly acquired.

1. Your boyfriend in kindergarten:
   a. Cute guy. Great colorer.
   b. Served as the resident back-of-the-school bus bouncer. *"Sorry, non-geekazoids only. Try another route."*

2. Your prom date:
   a. Rented a tux and borrowed his dad's Lincoln Town Car.
   b. Spent his life savings on a real tux (not a rental) and a white stretch limo.

3. Your college boyfriend:
   a. Went to the standard number of parties.
   c. Hosted (and still hosts) fetes with themes like Star Wars Pimps 'n' Hos and Jägercaust.

4. Your crush at your first job was:
   a. Someone you wanted to date.
   c. Someone you want to hate-fuck.

5. Your most recent date asked you about your:
   a. Favorite bands, movies, and TV shows.
   b. Company's org chart and whether he could get a copy for "research" purposes.

SCORING

MOSTLY A'S = YOU'RE SAFE
No Mrs. Big Stuff monogram for you. The guys you date aren't full of pomp and puffery. They're content with who they are: terrifyingly together and normal. We're guessing your bullshit detector runs like a Lamborghini or you used a time machine to skip over your early twenties. Either way, mazel tov!

MOSTLY B'S = YOU'RE OUT (BUT "IN" AT ALL THE HOTTEST NIGHTCLUBS)
You have an innate attraction to Mr. Big Stuffs. No need to be ashamed. It's nice when a guy has clean sheets and Burberry pajamas and can express an opinion without needing your repeated reassurances. Chances are you'll find a nice one on the lower end of the scale or else grow out of it in the next couple of years.

IF YOU DECIDE TO BOOK HIM FOR ONE NIGHT ONLY

aka the Ins and Outs of Being Friends with Benefits . . .

 *The Pros*

THE CHUCK BASS EFFECT

Once upon a time, there was a young man, popped of collar and pomaded of hair, a vision in seersucker and foppish neckwear of undetermined sexuality. His passion? To simultaneously titillate and repulse the ladies. Regular TV watchers might know him as Chuck Bass on *Gossip Girl*. The problem with this character is that he is, of course, a character. Boys like that do not go after girls like you. Fucking Mr. Big Stuff is fun because it's a way of bringing that fantasy to a more earthly fruition. All that bottled-up preppy lust had to come out somehow. So what if his Rolex is faker than the dialogue on *The Hills*?

THE AMENITIES

Mr. Big Stuff has nice living quarters. Unlike uptight art-director types, Mr. Big Stuff will not be irritated if you introduce a speck of dirt into his immaculate minimalist boudoir. He's more interested in seeing your naked bod. The lighting is perfect, the room temp is optimal, and there's no distortion in the sex-music speakers. It's like being in a hotel room. Which makes your fantasy of being a high-priced escort (or *him* being a high-priced escort) that much more believable.

THE CONFIDENCE

Out in public, Mr. Big Stuff's overstuffed ego is something of a liability, but in the bedroom his self-confidence is an asset. Some guys get so nervous they lie there mute. Mr. Big Stuff is so animated it's like he's giving an X-rated PowerPoint presentation. He *always* wins over his audience. It's a turn-on to be with someone who doesn't feel the need to cover his ass with a bedsheet when he gets up to go to the bathroom or apologize profusely every time he makes a minor blunder. Mr. Big Stuff truly believes he has the entire package, and he's proud of the package he has to offer.

THERE'S A SET POINT AND YOU DON'T GO PAST IT

Mr. Big Stuff is good at different kinds of the same sex and is able to adjust the speed and intensity: high, medium, low. However, exploring outside that zone makes him balls-crawling-up-the-ass nervous. Instead of admitting that he's never tried something, he'll change the subject by going down on you or employing some other old standby. You like old standbys, so you give in. Hence the sex never gets to the level it should be for a fuck buddy, which is too fuckin' bad.

HE GETS THE WEIRDS

Of all the guys you're going to date, pretend to date, or vagina date, this guy's pillow talk is the most revealing. Why? Probably because he spends so much of his time putting on a façade. You'll hear all kinds of stuff, most of which you wish he'd kept in lockup: his feelings for an untouchable model type, the circle jerks at high school rowing practice, how he once had a really vivid sex dream about Tony Romo. You did not sign up for this. As a girlfriend, maybe, but can't you just enjoy it for what it is without having to play amateur psychologist?

IT FEELS HOOKERISH

The night before, it felt hookerish in a good way. Now it just feels hookerish in a bad way. Which is surprising. You're generally sex-positive. (Dr. Ruth FTW!) Lately, you feel like there might be something wrong with you if you're good enough for the upper crust to roll around in the hay with but not good enough to be an actual girlfriend. Of course, Mr. Big Stuff could ask the exact same thing of you. Why is it that you would never consider him boyfriend material? But you'd never think of that, would you? Because that would be a calming thought, and you prefer to flood your neural passageways with as much anxiety as possible.

IF YOU DECIDE TO MAKE HIM THE HOUSE BAND

aka from Groupie to Girlfriend and Beyond . . .

 *The Pros*

MY PRETTY SHOW PONY

Do you ever get that urge to throw a bridle and an embroidered saddle blanket over Mr. Big Stuff that says *"Mine, fuckers!"* Of course you do. For this is a rarity. A write-home-about. You've had significant others who are impressive in their own way—they're up-and-coming musicians, unconditionally supportive partners, poor but sexually gifted improv artists—but few of them excel in such a universally accepted and quantifiable way. The kind of success that makes grandmothers and old high school friends stalking you on Facebook take notice. It's your fifteen minutes, so get him in as many family photos as you can. You may not get another chance to be the golden daughter.

NO SUPPLEMENTAL SUPPORT REQUIRED

You can find plenty of boyfriends who are more sensitive than Mr. Big Stuff. The catch is that you have to give them reassurance at every turn. You know how moms are with five-year-olds at the grocery store: "Go pick out a juice box!

Yes! That's a great juice box! Good for you!" What an aggravation. Fortunately for you, Mr. Big Stuff doesn't consult you on decisions. He just makes them. He doesn't ask you if you think he's hot shit. He already knows he is. It gets annoying sometimes (more on that in a bit), but in this era of sweater-clutching, doe-eyed emos, it's nice to see a bit of that vestigial swagger in a male human. As your grandma used to say, it's good for the ovaries.

HE CAN BE BY HIMSELF

The longer you're with someone, the more you realize that spending time together isn't necessarily in your best interest. While you're doing what you do, even if what you do is look at gossip sites until your retinas burn out, Mr. Big Stuff is off hanging with his boys or playing some sort of sport or wacking it to glossy home theater catalogues. In a new relationship you might feel a little threatened, but long term you'll dig the privacy and freedom. Mr. Big Stuff needs you. But not really. Is that unromantic? No. You'll discover around Year 5 or so that it's awesome.

The Cons

HE NEEDS TO SHUT HIS FACE

Why? Because he talks all the time and yet says nothing. Is it possible you've been in an Ambien fugue for the past eighteen months? You don't know what you're doing or how you got here. He doesn't believe anything you believe. You could live with that, if only he were respectful about it. He turns the relationship into a vaudeville act, with you playing the part of shrill girlfriend every time you bicker in public. It always gets a laugh from his friends but makes you feel like shit in the process. You've told him to stop, but it hasn't sunk into his patrician skull.

HE'S NOT RIGHT WITH HIMSELF

You're not right *your*self, what with your Benadryl habit and having to tap the side of the dining table a compulsive number of times before it finally "feels right" to eat dinner. Yet you do what people do when they have issues: bore your friend or pay a shrink to listen to all your whining. Mr. Big Stuff thinks all that's stupid. He's big on old-fashioned cures, like repression, willpower, and involuntary attitude adjustments. Bully for you, Mr. Big Stuff. I suppose that while you're waiting for your nontreatment treatments to take effect, the rest of us—including your girlfriend—will just suffer.

YOU CAN'T PRETEND ANY LONGER

You could give a fuck where people went to school or how well their record sales are doing or whether they're wearing some designer belt that costs a jillion dollars. That didn't take long, did it? The Date-a-Suit experiment is over. Every time you talk to one of his Ivy League friends, you visualize snatching the wine he's swirling (and swirling . . . and swirling . . why doesn't he fucking *drink* it already?) and downing it in one gulp. How long before the contempt breaks through? It's going to get awkward in here (like, first-bar-mitzvah-multiplied-by-human-resources-exit-interview level awkward) when you finally crack.

 Every Rose Has Its Thorn

HOW TO END IT HARMONIOUSLY

WITH A MOVING OF HIS CHEESE
Not familiar with the phrase? Check Mr. Big Stuff's bookshelf. It means changing routine, shifting plans, taking away a desired reward. Mr. Big Stuff is goal-oriented about everything, and he does not like *not* getting that which he believes he has worked for. You tell him it's over, his first thought is of the new micro-suede sofa ensemble. His second thought is what he's going to say about his lack of a plus-one at the annual company dinner. He may have spun a lot of sugar about loving you like he's never loved anyone, but shift the status quo and you'll see that protecting his investments and saving face come first. Always. This is not the kind of guy you ask for a break or a few days off. Once it's over, it's over.

WITH A BAD ATTITUDE
There's no need to roll your eyes at his Audi's new floor mats or make snide remarks. Mr. Big Stuff is like a dog: He can sense contempt in concentrations as small as 1 part per 2 million. The more energy you shift away from him and the less fawning you do, the more he'll start to see the two of you as incompatible. He'll get bitchier, which makes your job easier. Instead of wondering how you can give up a hot guy who makes 250K for an average-looking Kinko's manager with a heart of gold, you'll wonder why you ever thought the task would be hard.

Mr. Big Stuff

WITH A SMALL-SCALE REBELLION

Go against plan. Ignore the crew instructions and posted placards. Refuse to spend $600 in airfare to go to his acquaintance's hometown wedding, and tell him that spending $200 on a brushed-steel trash can is flat-out dumb. Do only what *you* want to do. In other relationships you probably started doing this a long time ago. The difference with Mr. Big Stuff is that he can talk you into anything. When it comes to convincing, he's a mastermind. Start acting like the person you were before you started dating, and Mr. Big Stuff will be hurt and angry. A man of action, he'll soon dump you if you don't get there first. Warning: He'll take the friends with him, but you can always make new ones.

HOW TO KEEP MAKING SWEET MUSIC TOGETHER

UPSCALE DOES NOT EQUAL UP YOURS

You know what's worse than a snob? A reverse snob. You know what's really amazing? Truffle oil. Before you look down your nose at Mr. Big Stuff for ordering *pommes frites* in lieu of tater tots, know that some things are well liked for a reason, that reason being that they're awesome. By continually looking for ways in which he's "putting on airs" and assigning some sort of judgment, you're putting on airs yourself and denying yourself the opportunity to have some new experiences and meet some interesting people. Just because someone dresses

Every Rose Has Its Thorn

head to toe in Brooks Brothers doesn't mean he or she is incapable of compassion or intelligent thought. Even scrubby-looking anarcho-hipsters will sneer down their noses at you as if they were in a country club if you walk into the wrong dive bar. Getting along with Mr. Big Stuff means giving up some of your precious "authentic indie" tastes and being more open-minded.

KNOW THAT HIS BARK IS WORSE THAN HIS BITE

What on earth makes him think that everyone in the restaurant wants to listen to his loud cell phone conversation about creatine supplements we'll never know. However, we do know that part of it stems from how he sees himself, which varies very little from how he saw himself as a child: not good enough, not cool enough, not handsome, fast, or skilled at the critical stuff, like kickball. Some people will express that insecurity by turning inward, hiding from people at social functions. Others will funnel it into good (or terrible) music or art. Mr. Big Stuff handles his insecurity by overcompensating, and once you realize that, your tolerance level will grow and you may even come to love Mr. Shit-Talker. He may run his mouth a lot, but the longer he's around you, the more he truly becomes himself. Which, incidentally, is not such a bad fellow.

REALIZE YOU'RE NOT SO DOWN-TO-EARTH YOURSELF, THERE, PAL

We are all unique, beautiful individuals, each of us annoying in our own right. What's that? You're not annoying? Of course you are. You may not blare club music from your car speakers or wear sunglasses indoors, but everybody's capable of being a lout. How many more times do you have to mention volunteering in that faux-humble and oh-so-casual way of yours? Twelve? Twenty? There are ways in which you're insulting and annoying people that you haven't even realized, and it's been going on since you were born. (Babies are the biggest Mr. Big Stuffs of all—so selfish and needs-focused.) When you get down on Mr. Big Stuff for being too brassy, remember that there's someone who thinks the same of you as well. Your fake humility and carefully inserted foreign travel references aren't fooling anyone.

FOR THE RECORD

aka Relationship Lessons from the School of Rock . . .

PEOPLE ARE COMPLEX

There's actually a personality attached to that cocky gentleman you made out with as a joke at the bar. Over time, you got to know him versus making fun of him behind his back while letting him pay for expensive dinners. You learned that he irons away his nervous energy. When he runs out of clothing, he'll iron yours. Once he even went after the dish towels. As shallow as he is, he's not one-noted. He watches BBC. He understands rudimentary feminist arguments. Look out—Koko the Gorilla is gaining on Jane Goodall.

 Every Rose Has Its Thorn

YOU WILL FINE-TUNE YOUR FILTER
We're not saying you'll never date another Mr. Big Stuff. You will, however, be better informed. The next blind date you go on, you'll do more Google stalking. You'll be able to determine whether a guy genuinely went to that Sonic Youth concert or whether he bought the T-shirt at Urban Outfitters. You will learn that a history of dating sorority girls is not a mere coincidence but evidence of the fact that a guy likes dating sorority girls. Most important, when a Mr. Big Stuff tells you that girls like you don't usually go after guys like him, you will believe him.

PATTING YOURSELF ON THE BACK IS NOT OPTIONAL
It could have been his car, his condo, or his screenplay deal with a major producer. Whatever it was, you went into the relationship thinking that Mr. Big Stuff was somehow better than you, be it smarter, funnier, richer, and/or cooler. But after a while, by nature of who Mr. Big Stuff is, he'll start to irritate you. Then you'll start to wonder if maybe the reason you're irritated is that you've never dated a successful guy. All the guys you date don't do squat. Maybe you're hardwired to like losers. Yikes. Here's the deal, though: Take away Mr. Big Stuff's cigar smoke and antique mirrors, and he's just a person. He may have the charisma required to rock the party, but you know enough to thank the host once it's over. Be proud of who you are. Even though it's not paying off monetarily, it's paying off spiritually. Besides, we hear your dollar goes way further in Nirvana.

YOUR MINI PRESS KIT

Mr. Big Stuff is the guy who...

- Makes fun of *Sex and the City* for being vapid but sees no irony in his enjoyment of *Entourage*.

- Suffers from severe social anxiety over others' perceptions of his car, TV, and/or smart phone.

- Calls you "a delightful tomboy" because you don't make daily use of stilettos and hot rollers.

- Tips the waitress obscene amounts on your first few dates, just shy of 9 percent thereafter.

- Genuinely subscribes to "lady on the street and a freak in the bed" as well as other sayings best confined to *Now That's What I Call Music...!* compilations and sexist bumper stickers.

★ ★ ★ Reviews

What Critics Are Saying About Mr. Big Stuff

"He'll put off proposing forever because the ring has to be this huge rock."

—Bree

"He was the heir to a jewelry fortune on one of the home shopping networks. He would freak out and be like 'I'm not happy in the relationship' or this, that, or the other. Then he'd buy me apology presents to get me back. It got me trips to Disney World, Chicago, and Italy and a lot of custom jewelry, most of which was engraved with 'I'm sorry.'"

—Amanda

"Everything he did was an attempt to change me. Class me up. He'd take me to cocktail bars when he knew I preferred dives. He'd turn off E! and put on The McLaughlin Group *on Sunday mornings."*

—Anne

THE BOY WITH THE THORN IN

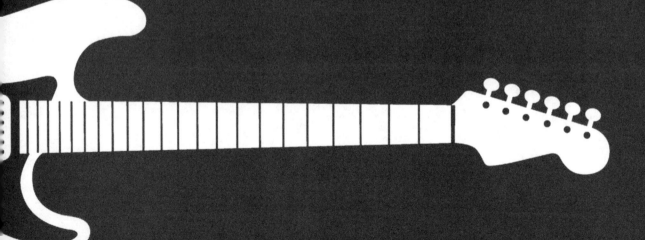

THE MEET & GREET

Who He Is

A moody ball of malcontent. A Publisher's Clearinghouse worth of issues. In the 1800s, probably would have died of something like lack of moxie or acute disinterest. The Brian Wilson of the Beach Boys. Every member of The Cure. The only one not smiling in the Six Flags roller-coaster photo.

What He's All About

The Boy with the Thorn doesn't have what most of us have, that is, an ability to temporarily shut out all the horrible. He can't just gnaw on a bagel, watch cat videos on YouTube, and accept that the most exciting thing that will happen to him all week will be discovering a new flavor of Vitamin Water. He's sensitive. Relentlessly anxious. His feelings are always close to the surface and raw. He's in touch with his emotions to the point where you wish he weren't. Does every feeling and passing thought warrant a four-hour discussion? To his credit, the Boy with the Thorn is also a superior emotional nurturer. Whether you need gooey affection, a kick in the ass, or hourly words of encouragement, Boy with the Thorn will bring it, and like some sort of Japanese super robot pet, he gets smarter and better at being with you the longer he's around. Like just about everything else that comes out of Japan, he's one part dark and strange, three parts adorable.

The Boy with the Thorn in His Side

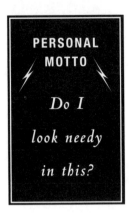

PERSONAL MOTTO

Do I look needy in this?

Turn-ons

Tears, monogamy, SSRIs, needing, being needed, fuzzy animals, abrasive ex-girlfriends, noncompetitive sports, layering, isolation, overthinking, journaling, masturbatory fantasies centered around being dominated by Parker Posey, diet soda.

Turnoffs

Public speaking, shaking hands with alpha males, drunk and rowdy groups of girls in halter tops, office karaoke, dressing rooms, gender-divided dinner parties, being left unattended, game day, formalized Pickup Artist methodology, forgetting his ear buds, large crowds.

THE HEADLINERS

Rock 'n' roll is great for bringing about joy and elation (see "Jump" by Van Halen), but it's also the theme music of anyone who's ever felt alone, unwanted, or unloved.

The following gentlemen have turned those feelings into a business enterprise. Meet a whiny British warbler, the world's most issues-ridden industrial musician, and a lo-fi savant who somehow manages to make Jeff Buckley sound happy-go-lucky.

 Every Rose Has Its Thorn

MORRISSEY

Who He Is
British singer-songwriter, former front man of The Smiths, proof that you don't have to play pop music or be a female Latino dance sensation or porn star to go by a mononym, spokesman for the mocked, ignored, and/or closeted.

What Makes Him Such a Boy with the Thorn in His Side
Has maintained decades of fame and filled nearly a dozen albums with lyrics about reading books and being bored. Has gotten into snits with everyone, including Johnny Marr, his former Smiths bandmate and as close as Morrissey will ever get to having an ex-husband.

> **Boy with the Thorn Highlights**
> - Either cannot or will not bring himself to choose a sexuality and therefore is able to retain the claim that he is rejected by everyone.
> - According to reports, stopped a concert at Coachella because the smell of "burning animals" was permeating his vegetarian nostrils.
> - Has gone away and come back more times than a pro ballplayer. Someone needs to feel needed. Luckily, most Morrissey fans would open a vein to prove their ardor.

"It's hard to be a man. . . . There's more to life than being macho— such an ugly word—which is something that I realized at the age of one."

Morrissey,
Details,
December 1992

The Boy with the Thorn in His Side

TRENT REZNOR

Who He Is
Prominent Gothic-American. Founding (and only known) member of Nine Inch Nails; curator of North America's largest collection of leather trousers. Engaged in musical side projects with names ranging from "Lucky Pierre" to "Tapeworm."

What Makes Him Such a Boy with the Thorn in His Side
Primary artistic shtick is to make everyone uncomfortable by airing his issues in every song, interview, publication, and video. Periodically drops out of music to go to rehab/have personal epiphanies and "nourish his inner aspect," à la Gwyneth Paltrow.

"Part of it is that I'm insecure. My face isn't on the album covers ever and won't be because I don't want to be on there with a bad haircut that'll look dumb in a couple of years."

Trent Reznor on his mysterious image, *Rock Sound*, April 13, 2005

Boy with the Thorn Highlights
- To judge from song lyrics, his favorite verbs appear to be *bleed, work, break, kill, stab, waste*—and those are just on the upbeat B-sides.
- A master of misanthropy and self-sabotage who encourages fans to steal music at his concerts. Takes people on Twitter seriously to the point of announcing that he was quitting his twitting.
- In recent years, has fulfilled every emo boy's secret forbidden dream of working out and getting buff. Here's to tears on your Bowflex.

Every Rose Has Its Thorn

ELLIOTT SMITH

Who He Is
Mister Misunderstood. Late indie rock martyr. Predictably troubled offspring of Bunny, a music teacher, and Gary, a psychiatrist. Writer and performer of "Miss Misery," which lost to Céline Dion's "My Heart Will Go On" at the 1997 Academy Awards for Best Song.

What Makes Him Such a Boy with the Thorn in His Side
Song lyrics cover all the D's: death, despair, drugs, dsuicide. Went to Hampshire College—a school so liberal it has a "Let's be cool about nonviolent conflict resolution" song instead of a "fight" song.

> "It's nice when people like what you're doing, but it's also weird. I guess it's just what happens when you have people paying attention to you."
>
> Elliott Smith, *Interview*, August 1998

Boy with the Thorn Highlights
- Started out playing sensitive-guy acoustic music during a time when all the public wanted was flannel-covered power chords.
- Suffered from lifelong depression and substance addiction, the latter of which got so bad that audience members had to help him remember his own lyrics from time to time.
- Changed name from Steven to Elliott because he thought the former sounded like a "jock" name.

The Boy with the Thorn in His Side

HIS REGULAR VENUES

aka Where You'll Find Him . . .

WITHIN FIFTY YARDS OF AN EX-GIRLFRIEND

Rarely is it a clean, efficient breakup with Boy with the Thorn. The path to separation is long and winding, filled with guilt-festooned birthday party invitations and "closure talks" that never seem to come to a close. Unlike other distraught exes, who will come to your door drunk and yelling swears, Boy with the Thorn will go through socially acceptable avenues to be around his ex–significant other. A good place to find him is at an engagement party his ex is throwing with her new fiancé or at a show, watching her play with the band he was kicked out of. Boy with the Thorn can handle it, he swears. He just needs to go into the bathroom and cry a little and maybe open the medicine chest and ponder whether Vicks VapoRub is deadly if ingested in sufficient amounts.

SOME MOPEY KIND OF SHOW

We're not going to limit Boy with the Thorn to any specific kind of music, although the most obvious genres that come to mind are shoegazer, new wave, and emo. The kind of music that makes you feel like the lead singer is singing only to you and gives you a deep pain in your chest and a golf ball in your throat. Look for the guy staring in rapt attention, with the look on his face like the little girl in *Poltergeist*. Although it seems like he's having a very personal, almost religious experience, Boy with the Thorn is actually very open to being approached. He's like a cult member: open for suggestion. Go for it, you shallow opportunist.

A CHEERFUL, COMMUNITY-TYPE GATHERING

Once in a while Boy with the Thorn will heed the advice of his friends/therapist/bank teller and try to do something productive and positive. He'll set his alarm for two p.m. and arrive at a neighborhood potluck, jam session, or clothing swap, which he'll quickly flee in terror when asked to wear a name tag or utter more than three syllables. If you want to meet him, you have two choices: Host one of these events (ew!) or crash one. The latter is cool because you can sit on the sidelines and no one will bother you, save for Boy with the Thorn. Join him in his misery, why don't you?

His Act

aka Ways of Working the Crowd . . .

ISOLATING HIMSELF

Certain thoughts go through a girl's mind when she sees a guy sitting alone at a bar. Is he trying to cultivate mystery (blech), an alcoholic (double blech), one of those creepy guys who thinks the bartender's actually interested in him (blech times infinity), or just new in town? The answer for Boy with the Thorn? None of the above. He self-secludes because that's how he's most comfortable. Particularly when he's upset, which is a lot. People hurt his feelings inadvertently: An offhand remark from his boss can prompt him to start saving for his inevitable unemployment; a girlfriend having a little "too" amazing a time talking to an old male roommate at a house party will put him outside on the front porch, shivering in the snow. New situations can also do this, as will new people and unfamiliar sights and smells. He's a bit like a cat in that way. He needs to be introduced *slowly,* or he'll hide under the radiator until you smell the singed fur and finally shoo him out.

PRACTICING SELF-CENSORSHIP

Blame Boy with the Thorn when the Wave gets broken at a stadium or the clapping at a rock show dies off. Blame Boy with the Thorn for dull wedding receptions and conga lines that disintegrate into nothing. Boy with the Thorn is not doing this deliberately. He's not a contrarian or incapable of having a good time. He just holds himself back a lot. He's so afraid of fucking up, being criticized or blamed or yelled at, or making a fool out of himself that he misses out on a lot of the fun.

DYING TO BE PICKED UP

When it comes to wanting to be swept off his vintage loafers, Boy with the Thorn is worse than a 1950s girl at the prom. He specializes in sidelong stares, doe eyes, and telegraphing *"Pick me—pick me—pick me!"* brain-wave signals while at the same time doing everything he can *not* to appear obvious. This often

Every Rose Has Its Thorn

has the net effect of making him look stuck up, sickly, and/or bored. As a result, in social settings, the majority of girls will put him in the Discard pile after giving him a quick once-over. The remainder will find him incredibly irresistible and endearing. Not at all a coincidence—these are the same girls who enjoy cultivating nervous plants and pets, like ferns and greyhounds.

His Wardrobe

aka Proper & Improper Attire . . .

Fig. 7b: Contents: hoodie, backup hoodie, sketchbook, pain.

THREADS LAID BARE

While it's true that black is favored by the overwhelming majority of Boy with the Thorns, as both a color and a cry for help, within this subset you'll find a variety of styles, from gloomy dandy to gloomy scenester to gloomy lumberjack. Impressing you is the thread that unites it all. Boy with the Thorn dresses well (or at least makes the attempt) because he wants your approval. Have you ever seen the couple where the girl is all dolled up in a sundress and high heels and the guy is wearing an "I got SH*TFACED at Señor Drunkenfrogg's '07!" T-shirt and cargo shorts? Boy with the Thorn and his lady friend are the precise mathematical opposite.

The Boy with the Thorn in His Side

WHAT HE WEARS

The Confidence Uniform
Actually, "confidence" might be overstating it. This is the combination of clothing that makes him feel like less of an unattractive freak loser. This usually leads to defensive dressing: buying multiple versions of the same outfit and wearing it day in, day out. The upside to the confidence uniform is that it was usually chosen with great care and therefore looks really good on him. The downside is that none of your friends believe he does laundry and it gets a little boring to look at after a while.

The Occasionals
These are outfits purchased by well-meaning female best friends, mothers, and anyone else who's ever tried to get Boy with the Thorn out of his Confidence Uniform. It also includes purchases Boy with the Thorn made in a state of extreme elation, whether it be because of the band getting back together or a new job. These "out there" items (a sweater vest instead of a sweater! a microscopic pattern! a lighter shade of charcoal!) get trotted out a couple times a year if consistent peer pressure is applied or if any of the above individuals comes over and goes through his closet.

The Never-Worns
Items that never leave the closet. They may have been found on top of the trash, purchased during a post-breakup psychosis, or accidentally bid on while surfing eBay drunk. Never-worns are the subject of much curiosity by girlfriends and

Every Rose Has Its Thorn

snoopy roommates. *What is this? Is he gay? A fetishist? What possible explanation could Mr. Black T-Shirt have for owning a pair of pink pleather trousers?* Upon discovery, Boy with the Thorn will become sheepish and withdrawn, resisting with uncharacteristic anger and resolve all inquiries and lighthearted requests for him to try it on.

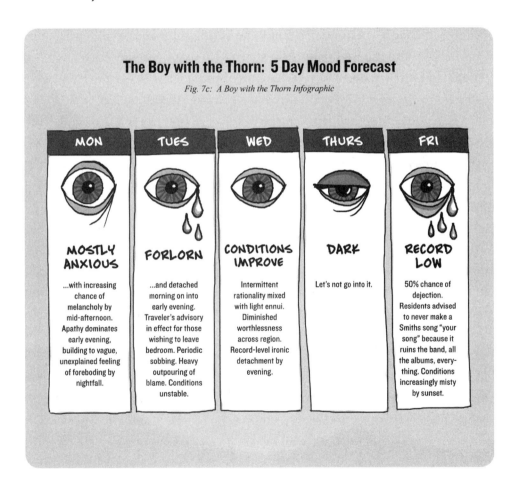

Fig. 7c: A Boy with the Thorn Infographic

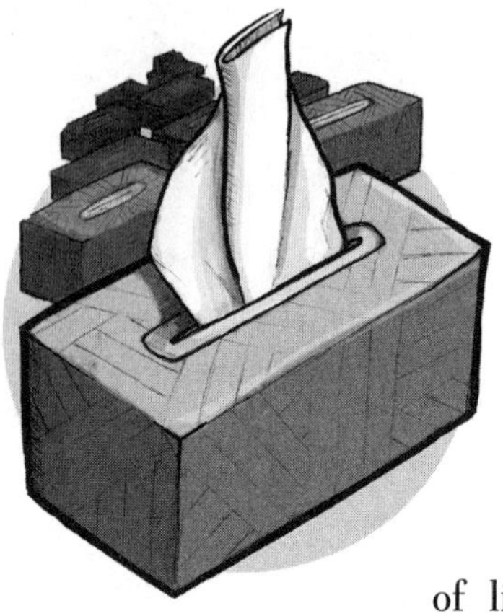

How to Get Backstage

or at the Very Least His Phone Number...

Fig. 7d:
Issues mean tissues.

BE BORDERLINE

That is, be in no position to be dating someone, whether by virtue of life situation—you're still sharing a one-bedroom with your ex-boyfriend, but it's okay because you share the same bed but "try not to" touch—*or* because you were recently hospitalized because you took a bunch of pills after your ex left, and started hallucinating birds in cages that weren't there. The next time you want to lose your shit, have at it. Break down and cry on a street corner. Have a panic attack in the middle of Sam's Club. Be like Kate Winslet in *Eternal Sunshine* and just automatically insinuate yourself into Boy with the Thorn's life in the role of girlfriend.

Why It Works

Being needed is the only thing Boy with the Thorn needs more than you. Many a girl (including, ahem, this book's creators) has been dumped by a Boy with the Thorn by simple virtue of having her shit in order. Who wants a girlfriend who can take care of herself and doesn't need financial or psychiatric intervention? That's no fun. How will he ever get to play brave martyr and soak up all those sympathy kudos if she never has a breakdown?

GET A GIMMICK

We're not recommending you enroll in some shitty class (enroll in some shitty class) or change anything about yourself (change everything about yourself). You're probably already doing one of the above as a matter of course. The key is packaging it and making it more visible to the public. Do you wear your painting clothes while painting? How amateur. Next time, leave them on when you go to get coffee. Better yet, on a first date. If you're making cupcakes topped with marzipan pandas in space suits and then consuming them alone instead of taking them to a friend's birthday where everyone can admire your generosity, talent, and frosting chops, then you might as well slap a sticker on your lapel that says "Hello, my name is Hopeless."

Why It Works

Boy with the Thorn is self-aware in many aspects except this: He is powerless against cute girls with quirks. Quirks like playing the ukulele or holding down day jobs as epidemiologists with the U.S. government. He considers himself a reject, so he sees other "rejects." While he may begrudge that smile you bring to his face, you can be certain your unique brand of cool will keep him coming back for more.

RUN ERRANDS IN INCLEMENT WEATHER

It's cold, windy, and pissy gray. The rain is doing that noncommittal drizzle. Enough to ruin the bangs you just straightened and get your sweater all clammy but light enough to make you look like a vain crybaby for whipping out an umbrella. Any other girl would stay inside and crack open a good tabloid or briefly consider going to the museum. Not you. You will go to the dry cleaner, the oil-change place, and the cobbler.

Why It Works

Boy with the Thorn loves unnecessary suffering. Going to get groceries (which can now be delivered) or going to get knives sharpened (his fridge is empty and there's nothing in the house to cut except himself) when it's fifteen degrees and hailing is the perfect (if you'll pardon the pun) storm. Seeing you, a spot of brightness against a cheery backdrop, is his ideal meet-cute. Not that he knows what a meet-cute is. He doesn't go to mainstream romantic comedies.

PLAYLIST

New Wave of Tears: Eighties-ish Songs for Boy with the Thorn to Sob To

1. **"Bizarre Love Triangle"—New Order, 1986, Factory**
   Nothing cheers like a cheery song about infidelity.
2. **"Tainted Love"—Soft Cell, 1981, Phonogram**
   Unless that something is another, equally cheery song about fucking around.
3. **"Add It Up"—Violent Femmes, 1983, Slash Records**
   A numerical recap of all the times you've let Boy with the Thorn down.
4. **"Boys Don't Cry"—The Cure, 1979, Fiction Records**
   But he will.
5. **"Shout"—Tears for Fears, 1984, Phonogram Records, Mercury**
   It's okay to initiate a relationship discussion at four in the morning. Tears for Fears said so.

The Boy with the Thorn in His Side

POP QUIZ

Feeling Through the Feelings with Boy with the Thorn

Feelings. We've all heard of them. Some unfortunate nonmedicated individuals may even experience them every once in a while. What better way to test whether your boy is a bona fide Boy with the Thorn or just a boy than by answering the questions below?

1. I know he's happy when he:
   a. Wants to go out late.
   b. Wants to go get the mail.

2. I know he's sad when he:
   a. Listens to weepy music.
   b. Listens to happy music, with the intention of making his misery that much starker.

3. I know he's feeling mushy when he:
   a. Leaves me cute Post-its.
   b. Leaves me hand puppets sewn into our likenesses from Popsicle sticks and felt.

4. I know he's feeling horny when he:
   a. Grabs my ass.
   b. Grabs my purse and offers to carry it for me.

5. I know he's feeling mellow when he:
   a. Puts on his pajama pants.
   b. Sleeps for four days.

6. I know he's feeling anxious when he:
   a. Keeps checking his alarm clock.
   b. Doesn't blink for seventy-two hours.

7. I know he's feeling safe when he:
   a. Pees while leaving the door open.
   b. Pees without making me leave the apartment.

8. I know he's feeling self-conscious when he:
   a. Crosses his arms in front of his chest.
   b. Clutches his chest and passes out.

9. I know he's feeling self-confident when he:
   a. Stands up straight, smiles big, and banters with strangers.
   b. No.

10. I knew it was meant to be when he:
    a. Told me he loved me.
    b. Told me about his stretch marks.

11. I knew it was over when he:
    a. Told me he was jealous of my male friends.
    b. Told me he was worried I was cheating on him even though we'd never gone out.

SCORING

MOSTLY A'S = BOY
Call in the cavalry. You landed yourself a normal. Neither excessively moody nor excessively cheery, this fellow has down days but usually lands on his Adidas. He's not an oaf, but don't expect him to take an interest in your Etsy project, either. He is what he is, and what he is can be pretty cool. It's certainly low-hassle.

MOSTLY B'S = BOY WITH THE THORN IN HIS SIDE
Break out the Puffs Plus with Empathy. Someone's going to need a lot of special handling. Have you ever wanted to date a lesbian but burst into laughter at the sight of a strap-on? Have you ever had a burning desire to share secrets, kitten JPEGs, skinny jeans, and Diet Coke? If so, meet your future husband.

IF YOU DECIDE TO BOOK HIM FOR ONE NIGHT ONLY

aka the Ins and Outs of Being Friends with Benefits . . .

 *The Pros*

HE HITS BOTH ANGLES

Boy with the Thorn is capable of drilling you all night *and* complimenting you over pancakes the next morning. He won't break out into hives and start formulating an escape plan if you get a little heavy-handed with the kissy-face snuggles. He likes it, probably more than a casual partner should. But wouldn't you rather have that than a guy who pulls out his phone while he's still in you?

HE GOT AN A IN FRENCH

Boy with the Thorn wouldn't be caught dead in a slogan T-shirt. If he *did* wear a slogan T-shirt, it would have "#1 KISSER" emblazoned on it next to a big glittery red lip print. Kissing generally loses its significance as we get older, but Boy with the Thorn still kisses like it's the only sexual act he's allowed. The pressure, the intensity—all of it is amazing. Often with fuck friends you have to sacrifice kiss quality. There's no use training someone if he's not going to be a permanent employee. Boy with the Thorn needs no instruction.

MY LIL' RELATIONSHIP

Don't have time for a full-on boyfriend? Rather chill with your friends? Not ready to pick a sexuality? With Boy with the Thorn, you can meet, hook up, fight, make up, fight again, and break up, all in a single hookup. What can we say? The guy's a moodster. You spend half your bedroom time naked, the other half naked and arguing. It's ideal for anyone who grew up the child of alcoholics. It also keeps you from getting too complacent. No one would ever move on—to another fuck buddy or a real relationship—if every bed were made of roses.

The Cons

REPEAT OFFENDER

You've told Boy with the Thorn that this is just sex. You like him, but you don't *like him like him,* and the two of you don't have a future. Boy with the Thorn plays along, even going as far as agreeing that it would "never work" and he's got "something going" with "this one girl" but can't remember her first name and is never able to provide any supporting detail. Whether it's "accidentally" leaving his journal open to an entry he wrote about you or leaving a social networking note that's essentially pissing all over your profile to mark his territory ("Looking into your eyes last night was amazing, my little mouse!"), Boy with the Thorn breaks hookup rules of etiquette left and right. Too bad there's not some sort of fine system—$50 for every drunken "I love you."

CUDDLE TROUBLE

Are you good at sleeping while holding hands? What about both hands? What about feet? Boy with the Thorn cuddles so close you can hear his cells dividing. This can get annoying even with someone you really love, let alone someone you have a limited tolerance for. You try for more physical space and you may get it for a second or two, but eventually he's stuck to you again. You'd swear the bed was tilted, and you wouldn't put it past him to saw off a leg to put the odds in his favor.

THIS IS A PORNO, NOT A TALKIE

Chatty, chat, chat. Boy with the Thorn likes to talk in bed. Unfortunately, very little of what he says is dirty. It's either borderline jealous and inappropriate ("Been on any good dates lately?") or just plain unrelated ("I've really been thinking a lot about existentialism"). A little vocalizing is nice. It's just that you'd rather the conversation be over bagels the next morning or making fun of something on TV when you flick it on afterward. You don't like having to feel like you're entertaining an out-of-town relative when you've just finished orgasming.

IF YOU DECIDE TO MAKE HIM THE HOUSE BAND

aka from Groupie to Girlfriend and Beyond . . .

 *The Pros*

HE'S EMOTIONALLY INTELLIGENT
More important than liking the same bands or having the same takeout preferences is how you react to people, events, and situations. You love going to parties with Boy with the Thorn and discussing them afterward, because he has the spot-on opinions about everyone you just met. You can be at the shittiest social gathering on earth—an office picnic obstacle course in 104-degree weather followed by a salt-eating contest—and it's better when he's there, because at least one person is thinking how you're thinking.

HIS NEUROSES HELP YOU OWN YOURS
Finally, a guy with your special house blend of issues. A guy who needs to be told he's handsome and feels a twinge of the jealous when he hears how your ex just got a record deal. Cooler still, he tells you about it. He lets you console him, and by doing so, you realize how ineffective and idiotic it is to worry about

such dreck. You feel like a savior or a shrink with a fancy office and tasteful teak sculptures. A nurturing Earth Goddess who warms hearts with her rose quartz–tinted wisdom and her homemade pumpkin soup served in hand-thrown tureens. You are less crazy because he's crazy. That kind of therapy is priceless.

HE'S REALLY INTO YOU

Boy with the Thorn told you he wanted to be your boyfriend within the first couple of days of meeting you. It wasn't long before he was assigning you nicknames and asking to take a "couple picture." Every time you think "Huh, I haven't heard from him in a while," he's at your doorstep or in your inbox. There is no nail-biting or wondering how long is long enough or should I/shouldn't I wait to send this e-mail. He says exactly what you want to hear, and, unlike smooth talkers you've had in your past, it's not bullshit when he says it. You are constantly pinching yourself. It's so good it can't be real. Oh wow. Here comes the segue . . .

The Cons

THE TROPICAL FISH FACTOR

Read all this and still want a Boy with the Thorn? We don't know. We'll have to talk to your father. We're not sure if you're ready for the responsibility. What's that? In order to thrive, Boy with the Thorn requires constant monitoring,

grooming, placating, kowtowing, and complimenting. He won't be happy with five-minute talks. You have to stroke his ego five times daily and change his compliments often. Are you ready for that? Yes, he's very beautiful to look at, we know.

HE WANTS TO BE UNHAPPY

The best girlfriend in the universe couldn't make this guy content. Boy with the Thorn is happiest when he has something to be unhappy about. Who asks not to celebrate Valentine's Day and then gets upset when he doesn't get surprised with a Whitman's Sampler? Who gets deeply offended when you suggest buying separate bottles of salad dressing, insisting that your inability to come to a resolution on this issue says something about the relationship? Boy with the Thorn takes everything as an omen, a bad one. Over time, you will eventually want to stop proving him wrong. You will become more and more okay with being a disappointment.

CONFIDENCE: IT'S NOT JUST FOR ASSHOLES

Before dating Boy with the Thorn, you thought self-confidence was a form of mental illness or at the very least an indicator of severe jackassery. You also thought you had no self-confidence. Come to realize you do; it's just a question of to what extent. Boy with the Thorn has a hard time asserting himself at the drive-thru. He cannot cope with the pressure of going to the bathroom during dinner and having everyone look at his "too flat" butt when he gets up to use the bathroom. His inhibitions are limiting. Say goodbye to dancing. Say goodbye to comedy shows (the comedian might point him out) and "would you rather" conversation games (in a roomful of lifelong friends he feels put on the spot). Boy with the Thorn creates a limited world for himself, and your world starts to feel cramped because of it.

HOW TO END IT HARMONIOUSLY

WITH PRIOR WARNING
In certain relationship situations it's probably all right to make a hasty exit. You may even be required to by law. However, we do not recommend a cut-and-run strategy for Boy with the Thorn. He's super invested and already thinks he's worthless. Your dumping him is only going to serve to heighten that further. You can't go from celebrating his birthday and leaving him little notes in his shoes to saying "We have to talk," then twenty-four hours later changing your Facebook status and slapping up a dating profile. It's far more humane to tell him you're having SD (Serious Doubts) and ask for the ol' T&S (Time and Space), resolving to a FD (Final Dump). This whole process should take a minimum of two weeks but no more than two months. Boy with the Thorn hates limbo as much as he loves suffering.

WITH A HEART-TO-HEART

We hear you. This one's a "duh." However, have you noticed how every relationship talk starts out with big plans? You've read some articles, talked to friends, and are ready to be composed, loving, communicative, and open. Instead, you wind up saying "like" and pausing for nine minutes between each "like," coming off like a time-delayed English-as-a-Second-Language version of a valley girl. That treatment? Not going to work this time, kiddo. Boy with the Thorn is going to expect more than "It's not you; it's me," and he's not going to be satisfied with "I'm not in love." He'll want every qualifying detail and thought, and you'll be torn as to whether or not to give it to him and ease his pain or protect him from it, kind of like some kind of Dear Abby meets Dr. Kevorkian.

WITH A COUPLE OF FLARES, SOME CANNED GOODS, AND A RAIN PONCHO

It's not our intention to scare you, but we have to be frank. We have no idea how this is going to go down. Boy with the Thorn is amazing to date. Out of all the guys in this book, he's one of the best. He knows how to say and do things that make you feel like the most singularly awesome woman on earth. In a way, Boy with the Thorn *is* Mother Earth: capable of making fuzzy baby chicks but also sending a tsunami to demolish Old McDonald's farm. He is emotionally attuned enough to be really good at hurting you. Will he? Or will he turn that hurt on himself? Tread carefully.

HOW TO KEEP MAKING SWEET MUSIC TOGETHER

DON'T FORCE HAPPY

Remember when your manager at Bennigan's used to tell you to smile, even as you were carrying a tray full of dirty ashtrays and chicken wing bones back to the kitchen and your ass was the only thing visible to diners? How awful was that guy, making significantly more than you and never having to touch a dirty dish, yet telling *you*, "C'mon, get happy!"? What a knob. That's how your unyielding cheer feels to Boy with the Thorn. Moods do not exist to be modified, cured, or judged. A smooth future with Boy with the Thorn rides on your ability to ride out the low peaks and still lower valleys without taking each one as a personal affront. We're not saying to put on a party dress and head out dancing when he's sobbing in the garage; we're just saying to be supportive but be quiet about it. It's like a two-year-old who falls down. A lot of the pain expressed depends on how others around him respond. If you act like a bad mood is the end of the world, it will be. Treat it casually, and he may soon be saying something positive.

YOU CAN SAY "BACK OFF"

At first it feels incredible to be inundated with tokens of affection, but after a while you feel smothered by all the daily love notes and handmade collages. Being in a lasting relationship with Boy with the Thorn may mean you start to take this stuff for granted. Bad call. Without proper maintenance, you'll break his spirit like they did in that horse movie and ruin your Boy with the Thorn. Tell him when too much is too much. You won't be karmically "Be Careful What You Wished For!" punished. Promise.

CELEBRATE NEURO-DIVERSITY

You may not understand his moods and may think he's way too sensitive, but isn't it comforting to know that there are men who have complex emotions and, despite all the *Everybody Loves Raymond* and Mars–Venus propaganda campaigns, the mainstream media does not own the copyright to human gender roles? Feel what it's like to be the so-called guy for once. The good parts—like not stressing yourself out over every little thing—and the bad parts—getting called insensitive, feeling guilty, feeling like you're in the doghouse. The insights gained from having Boy with the Thorn as a boyfriend will give you perspective. It's as close as you can get to being the opposite sex without risky surgery in Taiwan.

FOR THE RECORD

aka Relationship Lessons from the School of Rock...

YOU WILL BE MORE APPRECIATIVE OF PAST BOYFRIENDS

Who knew communicating was so exhausting? That it's possible to go for forty-eight hours without having a status talk? Cell phones aren't supposed to be tethers, and it's possible to have an independent thought or action without having to call your sweetie and tell him all about it. All that neglect you complained about in previous relationships seems like such a waste of hot air. "Right to Privacy" is your new cause, and compared to Boy with the Thorn, everyone is low maintenance now. A guy who doesn't talk? Sounds perfect! A guy who doesn't share feelings? Bring it on! At least until you grow jaded again and resume complaining about what you don't have but really, really want.

THERE IS NO RELATIONSHIP-BY-JURY

Your friend may chastise you for not appreciating Boy with the Thorn. She's never known the joy of a being given a pet name or an unsolicited compliment. She's never been surprised with cute Japanese dolls shaped like sushi or heard her boyfriend confess that he changed shirts four times prior to their first official outing. Then here you are, having all of that and treating it not like a precious gift but like a burden. How dare you? Here's why: That friend's never had to date Boy with the Thorn. She doesn't see the bad, only the idealized good. Never let a friend persuade you to stay in something for her sake. This is not a threesome.

YOU'RE A LITTLE SELFISH. WHO KNEW?

Mom worried a little when you cut the hair off Barbie and drew pubes on Ken and tattoos on Skipper with a Crayola marker. She figured you'd grow out of it and become more balanced and nurturing when you were older. But have you? Being with Boy with the Thorn has made you realize how much work is involved in all of this relationship crapola. Maybe you're ready, maybe you're not. Right now, all you know is, Boy with the Thorn's teary calls are going to have to wait until you're done with this bath, really good bottle of wine, and dish of olives.

YOUR MINI PRESS KIT

The Boy with the Thorn in His Side is the guy who . . .

- ✦ Gets hives instead of a hard-on at the thought of you having a threesome.

- ✦ Has more pictures of your cats than you do—on his cell phone.

- ✦ Looks for deeper meaning behind every bit of activity on your Facebook profile.

- ✦ Makes you come to despise cuddling.

- ✦ Calls you back when you forget to say "I love you" before ending a phone call.

- ✦ Clings to your leg at social gatherings like a two-year-old.

★★★ Reviews

What Critics Are Saying About The Boy with the Thorn in His Side

"He's usually hung up on exes, past mistakes, and relationship issues that are easily solvable. Exhausting!"

—Kelly

"He had all these dreams but would never do anything about them. He'd be like, 'I don't know why anyone doesn't like my drawings,' and I'd be like, 'Well, did you ever show anyone your drawings?'"

—Lori

"He tried to kill himself by taking Tylenol because I didn't want to take him to the prom."

—Samantha

SWEET CHILD O'

MINE

8

Fig. 8a: Sweet Child O'Mine

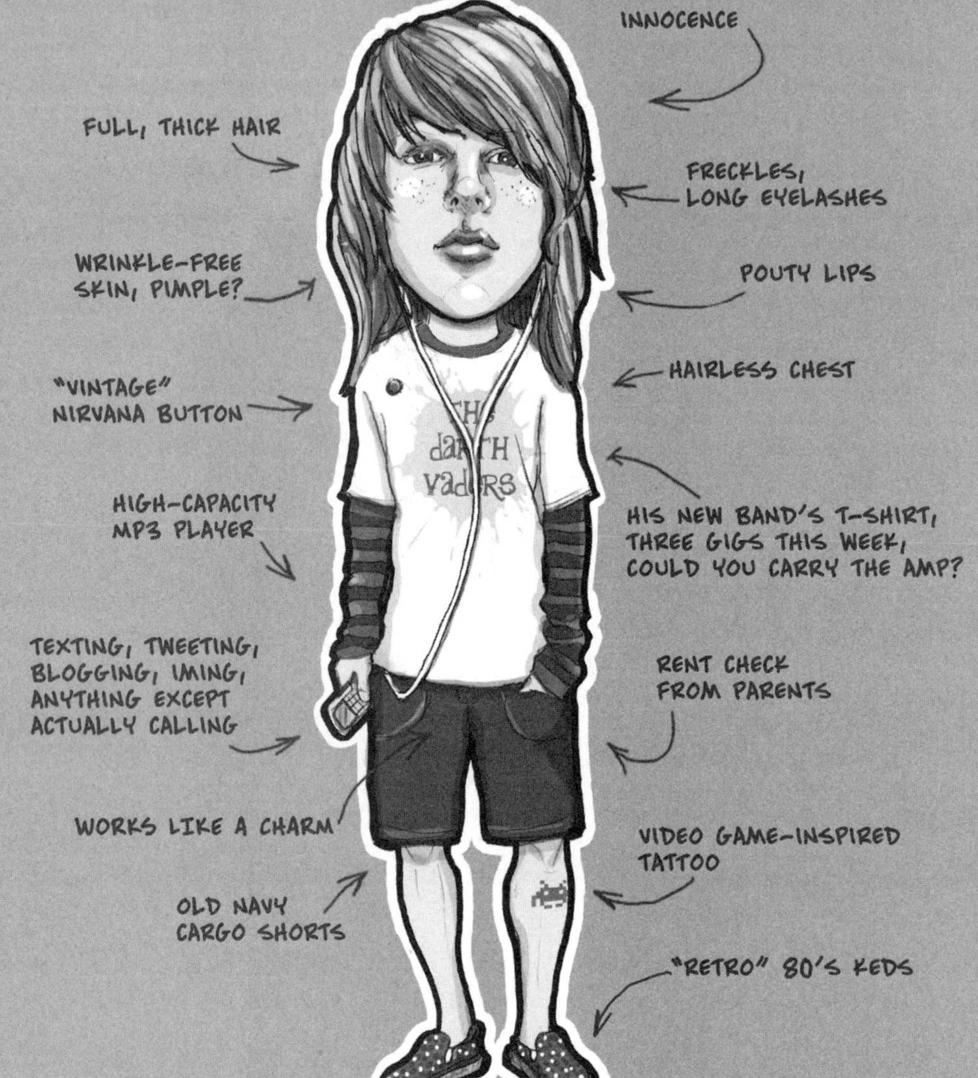
INNOCENCE
FULL, THICK HAIR
FRECKLES, LONG EYELASHES
WRINKLE-FREE SKIN, PIMPLE?
POUTY LIPS
HAIRLESS CHEST
"VINTAGE" NIRVANA BUTTON
THE darTH vaders
HIGH-CAPACITY MP3 PLAYER
HIS NEW BAND'S T-SHIRT, THREE GIGS THIS WEEK, COULD YOU CARRY THE AMP?
TEXTING, TWEETING, BLOGGING, IMING, ANYTHING EXCEPT ACTUALLY CALLING
RENT CHECK FROM PARENTS
WORKS LIKE A CHARM
VIDEO GAME-INSPIRED TATTOO
OLD NAVY CARGO SHORTS
"RETRO" 80'S KEDS

THE MEET & GREET

Who He Is

A boy among men. The reason hackneyed phrases such as "I don't usually do this" and "He's really mature for his age" are suddenly coming out of your mouth. Unproven in wisdom and complexity but rich in sexual energy and hair follicles. A master sommelier (Jennifer Aniston? Madonna?) would describe him as "charming and refreshing, with notes of Boone's Farm and acoustic guitar solo. Awkward finish, with an adorable button nose."

What He's All About

Old enough to take out in public, young enough to be in a different age bracket in an online drop-down form. Sweet Child o' Mine is hold-your-breath gorgeous, but, even more important, he's barely dipped a toe in the dating pool. This isn't about purity. The sluttier, the merrier. But unlike the other guys you've been dating, Sweet Child's not the least bit bitter, weird, or cynical. Although well intentioned, Sweet Child o' Mine's worldview is as unrealistic as his plan to breed pet-sized giant squid and make millions by starting an accompanying blog and social networking site about it. He thinks everything that comes out of his mouth is deep, claims to be a "huge '80s culture fan" but has never seen an episode of *The Cosby Show*, and preaches about the importance of self-reliance as espoused by Emerson and Thoreau while remaining firmly on Mom and Dad's payroll. Sweet Child o' Mine is like a *Tiger Beat* pinup come to life: dreamy and fun to stare at, if not a little two-dimensional.

Turn-ons

Chilling, being late, inaccurate retro, insta-friendships, organized irony, abandoning projects, finding meaning where there is none, famous old people, mistaking a passing interest for being "obsessed with" something; being complimented on his facial hair progress.

Turnoffs

Day jobs, overdue papers, being teased about his age, buying things he could BitTorrent, artificial sweetener, stories from your past, your drunk and letchy friends, Diane Rehm on NPR, paying extra for convenience or comfort—why take a taxi when you can bike in the rain and save $20 in beer money?

> **PERSONAL MOTTO**
>
> *Age ain't nothing but a number I don't have to worry about for at least ten years, possibly more.*

THE HEADLINERS

Rock 'n' roll is and will always be about youth. There's just something about newy, dewy, and naïve that's so ungodly appealing. Some social scientists say women prize power and security over good looks and sexual novelty. Yeah, right. And R. Kelly reads *CosmoGirl* for the articles.

Every Rose Has Its Thorn

Here now is a selection of past and present-day Sweet Children. Rip open a ring pop and enjoy.

NEW KIDS ON THE BLOCK

Who They Are
An all-boy bubblegum band out of Boston with members both sweet (Joey, Jonathan) and savory (Donnie, Danny); protégés of Maurice Starr, the record industry's answer to P. T. Barnum; living clip art for a multizillion-dollar merchandising franchise.

What Makes Them Such Sweet Children
Posable limbs and fluffy, combable hair; eyelashes longer than Sophia Loren's; equal ratio of moms and teens at concerts.

"The mothers love us just as much as the kids do."

Joey McIntyre of New Kids on the Block, interview on the set of video for "This One's for the Children"

Sweet Children Highlights
- *"We're gonna put you in a trance with a funky song!"* is most threatening lyric.
- Their NKOTB hotline (only $2 for the first minute!) logged over one hundred thousand phone calls per week during its prime.
- No longer young, but still easily influenced into bad decisions, as evidenced by their consent to a reunion tour.

THE JONAS BROTHERS

Who They Are
Three brothers who built their brand on faux pop punk and contractually obligated virginity; Disney starlet womanizers; another reason to hate on New Jersey.

What Makes Them Such Sweet Children
Perfect hair, perfect eyes, perfect little outfits; smiles so winning they could coax a smile out of a woman's prison warden; good intentions out the yin-yang.

Sweet Children Highlights
- Rose to popularity on the Disney Channel, presumably starting with captive, drooling infants in baby swings and working their way up the age ladder.
- Have performed alongside such controversial artists as the Muppets and Hannah Montana.
- Answer hard-hitting questions like "Do you have any pets?" and "Do you ride amusement park rides?" on their band website.

> *"When women can cook, that's always good! Guys like to eat."*
>
> Joe Jonas of the Jonas Brothers on what's sexy, *InStyle*, June 2009

Every Rose Has Its Thorn

JUSTIN TIMBERLAKE

Who He Is
Boy band 'N Sync's former lead singer; singer and dancer; former member of the Mickey Mouse Club; honorary member of the black community (currently on indefinite probation).

What Makes Him Such a Sweet Child
Legendary baby blues; white Chiclet baby teeth and cherub curls; suffers from Dick Clark syndrome, whereby he will always look twenty, even when he's fifty.

"I used to think I actually was Batman."

Justin Timberlake, *Time for Kids*, November 11, 2002

Sweet Child Highlights
- Total cougar bait for the older ladies: Courtships include Alyssa Milano and Cameron Diaz.
- Is sweet, but refuses to be anyone's dummy. Wrote scathing lyrics of "Cry Me a River" after betrayal by pop star Britney, who threw her life and hair weave down the toilet shortly thereafter.
- Young enough to revive trends that should stay dead and gone, i.e., leisure suits and beatboxing.

His Regular Venues
aka Where You'll Find Him . . .

AT A ROCK SHOW YOU KNOW NOTHING ABOUT
You went with your friend who has way cooler taste in music. She would never deign to take you, except that she and her boyfriend got into a fight at IKEA a couple hours before. The opening band's too loud, the drinks are expensive, and you have to be at work by seven a.m. to write your List of Goals and One-Year Action Plan for the job you ponder quitting every single morning. The only thing this shitshow has going for it is Sweet Child, who is staring at you from across the bar. You can go over and talk to him, but know that doing so means getting invited to the three shows he plans on attending after this with his roommate and his roommate's friend and this one girl named Sylvia, whom he doesn't know that well but who seems really cool and is from Belarus. Want to go?

AT A BIZARRE HAPPY HOUR
This is not the typical three-drinks-and-then-you're-off-to-watch-DVR-and-eat-Bac-Os kind of engagement. We're talking about happy hours that turn into happy evenings, happy late evenings, and happy past midnights. Soon it becomes unclear how you got there. Something about the jukebox and this one girl shouting and this old guy with a Santa hat and shots that taste like chocolate-covered pretzels. The next morning your coworkers are teasing you about being a "mouth

Every Rose Has Its Thorn

slut," and you're not sure what you did or whom you did it with, when you get a misspelled text that looks a lot like a 419 spam: *Hi honi! How r u love?* Then you realize: Holy shit! It's Sweet Child.

AT A SPONSORED PARTY

The kind thrown by manufacturers of alcohol and cigarettes, radio stations, and the occasional nonprofit. You're there for the free booze or because your mom told you to do weird things to meet men and this Den of Strange certainly qualifies. Everyone has a look. That look is ugly. The drink line is a million miles long, there's bad house playing and girls limping around in Lucite heels doling out test tubes full of caffeine-infused pink vodka. But look what we have here. It's Sweet Child, barbacking to make extra cash. Soon he will fall in love with the only girl in the room who understands what's wrong here and—unlike the million Mystic Tanned bimbos who've been hitting on him all night—can articulate it in a witty invitation for when he gets off.

His Act

aka Ways of Working the Crowd . . .

PLAYING WITH HIS THINGY

Not that thingy, you pervert. We're talking about his music player, navigation device, and/or smart phone. Not because he thinks it looks cool. It's an everyday necessity. You don't get all showboat using a toilet or a knife and fork. Even more than you, Sweet Child is used to knowing exactly what everyone in his friend group is thinking, doing, and planning on doing at any given moment. Not only that, but what they'll be doing twenty minutes from now. Is it cooler than whatever he's doing at this precise moment? Yes, sex, as well as the possibility of having it with you, is cool, but he's had access to the most f'd-up adult material since grade school. What could be more important than accepting this invite to a Mötley Crüe–themed flash mob? When Sweet Child gets a little older, he'll realize that divided attention is not the best way to get the ladyfolk. For now, you'll have to text him a greeting, even if you're standing two feet over.

WAITING IN THE BOOZE LINE

Why anyone would wait a half-hour for Snickers vodka is beyond your comprehension, but that happens to be the official free libation for the evening, and Sweet Child is still of the age in which he feels like he's being offered an unbelievable opportunity to get in on the ground floor. Wise women know not to approach Sweet Child before he's gotten his alcohol. If you do, he'll be indifferent at best. At worst, he'll be annoyed at you for attempting small talk and breaking his focus. Until he gets that glass object filled with ethanol in his tiny little paws, he's got eyes for only one woman, and that's the bartender, even if she's sixty and looks like she moonlights in poultry processing.

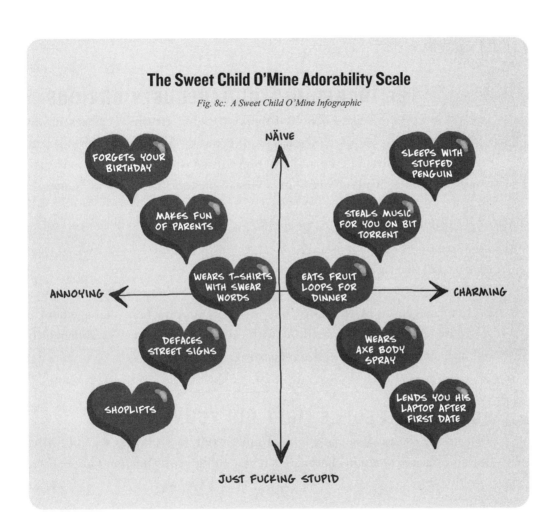

How to Get Backstage

or at the Very Least His Phone Number . . .

Fig. 8d: Contents: A $50 garlic press means you're an adult. An adult who does not own drinking glasses or bedsheets.

BE INCREDIBLY, RIDICULOUSLY OBVIOUS

You've seen *Three's Company*, right? In the seventies it wasn't about subtle. Take a lesson, if not an STD, from that era and go up to Sweet Child and give him a disco wink.* Once he's in the strike zone, buy him a drink or dish out a classic pickup line, such as "Come here often?"

Why It Works

This kind of directness is going to make you the ultimate Ms. Sophisticate. He doesn't have to know that your day job is in supply-chain management and you're too modest to wear anything with exposed arms. You've established yourself as badass. Now you can keep coasting.

HAVE YOUR PEOPLE MEET HIS YOUNG PEOPLE

Sign up for the next slot at the pool table while he's playing a game with his friends or ask to share his barbecue pit at a public park (*You don't mind, do you?*

---

*A move used as part of courtship ritual. Involves a broad smile, a shampoo-commercial-worthy shake of the hair, and the exaggerated blink of one ocular.

 Every Rose Has Its Thorn

The grill over there has what appears to be a dead rat or a very furry baked potato wrapped in aluminum foil. What's your name? . . .). Make sure there's booze, a game involving some sort of ball, or some sort of moving picture on which to direct your focus. Mixed groups function best when there's a safety net available—something that can fill in the gaps of awkward small talk.

Why It Works

Sweet Child is used to functioning in groups of people of both sexes who influence one another's tastes and opinions. Marketers call them tribes. They use one another's input to validate and inform decisions. Once you get approval from his group, it's smooth sailing.

HANG OUT IN A HOUSEWARE STORE

Note we said *house*ware, not *hard*ware. There's a big difference. The latter is full of construction workers, DIY moms, and married dudes picking out storm windows. The first is full of arguing couples, yes, but it's also full of Sweet Children looking to furnish their first apartments. Don't try to educate Sweet Child your first pass. Instead, make it easy for him to display what an adult he is by asking for his advice on dish drainers. After he's comfortable, you can go on to point out the halogen lamp mistake in his cart or the bath rug that will disintegrate upon exposure to water, air, or bathroom lighting. (See Fig. 8d.)

Why It Works

Sweet Child loves his generation and his cultural references, but he's also impatient to prove to the rest of the world that he's a grown-up. To him, that translates to having quasi-nice housewares. Those who've gotten a little more grown up know that it's more about keeping a month or two's salary in the bank, being patient in the face of epic douchery, and going to work each day and pretending you're dumber than your boss. He'll find that out later. For now, he'll invite you to dinner because he's horny and into using his new pasta fork.

 **Every Rose Has Its Thorn**

PLAYLIST

Tease Me, Please Me, Loan Me Twenty Dollars:
Sweet Child and the Lovers Who Love Him

1. **"Maggie May"—Rod Stewart, 1971, Mercury**
   Just your average college summer romance: Boy meets prostitute. Boy loses prostitute. Instead of dropping out, boy gets bummed out and goes back to school.
2. **"Mrs. Robinson"—Simon & Garfunkel, 1968, Columbia**
   You're trying to seduce him. If your rack shirt and top-shelf liquor don't do it, this song will.
3. **"Maneater"—Hall & Oates, 1982, RCA**
   Your average Sweet Child wasn't even alive when this hit the Top 40. Enjoy his unique take on the garbled chorus: "She's a . . . *Mag Needa? Band Leader? Hand Cheetah?*"
4. **"Stacy's Mom"—Fountains of Wayne, 2003, Virgin**
   Little-known fact: Childless individuals can substitute their cat or dog's name for "Stacy" and still retain the original meaning of the song.
5. **"Hot for Teacher"—Van Halen, 1984, Warner Music Group**
   The anthem for all grad school TAs who've ever accidentally hooked up with one of their students.

POP QUIZ

Sweet Child o' Yours?

Ever asked yourself this question? Then look no further than around your special dudefriend's apartment.

Part I. The Haves

Give him one point for each of the following items currently in his possession:
- More than one pillow
- More than one bath towel
- Dress shoes less than five years old
- Condoms (add a point for twelve-pack or larger)
- Spare set of keys
- Living room with more than one place to sit down (add a point if neither is a bean bag or folding chair)

Part II. The Have-Nots

Give him one point for each of the following items *not* in his possession:
- Glow-in-the-dark ceiling stickers
- Bagel Bites
- Personalized products with names other than his own (Fred, Bernice, etc.)
- A TV or stereo setup that costs more than his yearly income
- Plastic sports sandals (Adidas, Nike, Teva, etc.)
- Someone named Sweet Tim sleeping on the sofa

SCORING

SWEET CHILD O' MINE (0–6)
Oh, baby. No. Seriously. This guy's an infant. But that's okay because you connect on a spiritual level, and he's an "old soul." If you want to know what that means, ask Michael Douglas.

SWEET CHILD O' GIVE-IT-TIME (7–14)
What's that Britney Spears song? "Not a Girl, Not Yet a Woman"? We've got the same situation here. Not a Grown Ass Man but not quite a Sweet Child. If you're a commitmentphobe, that probably scares you. But if you're immature for your age and looking for someone you'll grow into, he just might be your guy.

IF YOU DECIDE TO BOOK HIM FOR ONE NIGHT ONLY

aka the Ins and Outs of Being Friends with Benefits . . .

 *The Pros*

HE'S FABULOUS IN BED

His dick works, and he has tons of energy—but not in a creepy coke-snorting, clandestine-Viagra-popping, middle-aged LA guy with something to prove kind of way. His body is A-fucking-*mazing*. We're not necessarily talking muscles; a lot of Sweet Children aren't gym rats. It's more that new-car kind of unused smell that evokes power and luxury and all the things that people who own Bentleys take for granted, like little shampoos and gourmet pillow chocolates and obsequious bellhops.

NICE SKIVVIES

He still cares enough to wear good underwear, even though the rest of his wardrobe is pretty inconsistent. When he sits on your bed in his hoodie and colored briefs he looks like an American Apparel model, and it's so *perfect* your memory takes a snapshot because you know you will never be with a guy this hot again and that thought fills your vagina with ennui. She's started watching black-and-

 Every Rose Has Its Thorn

white foreign films, sipping espresso, and wearing black silk undergarments. You told her you'd do your best to make this last, but you don't think she believes you.

HAVE PENIS, WILL TRAVEL

He's cool about coming over to your house for a hookup. No matter where he is, even if it means schlepping over in the middle of a blizzard or coming straight from a red-eye flight at the airport. It's refreshing to see someone who's still so excited about sex and willing to travel for it. Guys your age are generally more into their DVR or work, with sex hovering between a two and a three on their priority list. It's nice to have someone who prizes a booty call over inclement weather.

The Cons

NAP TIME

It's hard to come up with one, but if forced to we'd say the sex is a tad vanilla. He's not experienced or comfortable enough to be into anything kinky. But then again, who needs big honkin' rubber dildos and personal lubricants (you know, as opposed to impersonal lubricants) when you've got such a fine specimen of almost-man in front of you? Who are you, John Waters? If this isn't good enough, what's it going to take? Dropping E and throwing mashed potatoes at each other in bunny suits? Come on, now.

HE BRINGS ON NUDIE-TIME INSECURITIES

The older you get, the more you realize most guys could give a rat's A about lingerie or scented candles. It's the body that's the main act. Only now you're with someone who's been seeing a different kind of main act. You know the one. If they were an '80s pop duo they'd be called Tauter & Younger. You feel compelled to step up your game but don't have the time or money for a new gym membership. Instead, you dim the lights and try to remain hopeful.

AWAY GAMES ARE NOT AN OPTION

The reason Sweet Child is cool about coming over is that his own place looks like a homeless shelter. Last time you went to his house you wanted to yell *"You are a bad man!"* and *"Not going to scary bad place! You can't make me!"* It looks like the "after" shot of the house on the corner that the police busted open and found a bunch of feral cats and empty Long John Silver's containers stacked to the ceiling. It's a bit much to deal with, even for a hookup.

Every Rose Has Its Thorn

IF YOU DECIDE TO MAKE HIM THE HOUSE BAND

aka from Groupie to Girlfriend and Beyond . . .

 *The Pros*

HE ISN'T ALREADY "OVER" EVERYTHING

Sweet Child is the opposite of jaded. Sweet Child still believes in goodness and democracy. He hasn't looked at the nutritional information on ramen noodles and realized they're the pasta equivalent of cigarettes in terms of carcinogens and chemicals. He believes in the possibility of responsible credit-card ownership, most urban legends, that his friends from college will be his friends forever, and that there's nothing creepy about popping in on your neighbors to invite them over for some barbecue and beers.

HE DOES WHAT YOU SAY

Sweet Child will go anywhere and do anything with you, which makes the dating process like Nutella washed down with fine cognac, i.e., excessively smooth. He's extremely malleable and all about your plans and fitting into them. You just have to ask. He can have a fab time just about anywhere. You get the feeling it will always be this fun with him as your boyfriend, and fun is good.

HE'S A CLASSIC NEUTRAL

Sweet Child isn't overflowing with life force, verbal treatises, prejudices, hardened stances, rants, raves, or opinions. He has an openness about him, a blank-slateness that makes you feel calmer around him. He's like a warm eggshell in a room with high ceilings: all-purpose, attractive, classy, an easy solution, and an excellent backdrop for whatever mood you're in. Neon green may be fun short-term, but it's not a good choice for a long-term boyfriend.

The Cons

GROWING PAINS BY PROXY

The opposite of jaded can also be translated into clueless and naïve. It's weird feeling like you're holding someone's worldview in your hands. It's also strange feeling like a fist-shaking curmudgeon before you even have a real front yard. You're reminded of the pains others took to not tell you there is no Santa Claus when you were little, and when he tells you of his plans to quit his paying day job and throw all his time and resources into opening some bar with his friend, which he knows will take off, and you know will not, you feel the same strain.

BEING THE ONLY ONE WITH A CONSISTENT SCHEDULE GETS OLD

There are days when you work fifteen hours, and you really want nothing more than to not think. If food appears in front of you, you will eat it. If a drink appears in front of you, you will drink it. If friends arrive, you will make conversation. Yet he's brimming with energy because he didn't have to work at his part-time job or has a week before his next major exam or a month before he heads off on his sojourn to Europe. Not only does this exhaust you, it also makes you resentful.

YOU NEED MORE OF A CHALLENGE

Sweet Child is a doll, but most aren't intellectually complex enough to sustain your interest long-term. It's the difference between a ten-thousand-piece puzzle and the one with five big wooden pieces. Horse. Duck. Cow. Pig. Chicken. Whew, that was fun. What's next? Oh yeah, that's right. *Nothing*. Sure, there is many a Sweet Child who is smart and engaging and intellectually stimulating as all get-out. The problem is that they're spread out all over and not all of them are into dating older women. Then you factor in stuff like they don't hang out in the same places you do, or they do but arrive four hours later, and the odds are going to be against meeting one of these and more toward one of the ones we described earlier. Sorry.

HOW TO END IT HARMONIOUSLY

WITH A DAY PLANNER

Sweet Child probably smokes a lot of pot. If he doesn't do that, he drinks. If he doesn't drink, he reads or games. For ten hours at a clip. He only has room for so many items in his memory. Start calling less and being less available, and chances are you'll slide to the bottom of his list of priorities. Pack your schedule solid so you're unavailable even if it does occur to him to give you a ring. Lather, rinse, repeat. Yes, it's pretty wormy, and it's terrible when others do it, but it's hard to feel sorry for someone with zero doubt and flawless skin who's still on Mom and Dad's payroll. He has some hurt coming to him. Why not teach the kid a lesson about life? It's going to happen sooner or later.

WITH AN EXCUSE

Because you're older, Sweet Child views you as a complex person with all sorts of past lives and secrets. You can make up some excuse about an ex-boyfriend (or girlfriend!) coming back or a new job that demands complete and total celibacy, and he'll probably buy it. Even if he doesn't, he's too preoccupied with finals to go and check out your story. Sweet Child will just assume you had issues, and will years from now affectionately refer to you as "that older chick I dated for a while."

WITH THE (GASP) TRUTH

Tell Sweet Child that it's not working. You're not into him the way he's into you, and this arrangement is no longer working for you, whether it's because you want a commitment or because you're tired of having to provide context for every cultural reference. (*Who hasn't heard of Sylvester Stallone?*) Sweet Child is a lot more developed than you give him credit for. He'll be able to roll with it, though he may send you a few needy texts in the coming weeks.

HOW TO KEEP MAKING SWEET MUSIC TOGETHER

STOP INTERNALIZING SOCIETY'S AGEIST BULLSHIT

In 99 percent of Sweet Child couplings, Sweet Child isn't the one worried about it; you are. You absorb media at the typical modern rate of one zillion parts per hour and can't help noticing that women who date younger men are made fun of and compared to predatory wildlife, while men who date younger women slip by without notice. Sweet Child doesn't want you to move the iron pills and fiber supplements to the back of the medicine cabinet. He doesn't want you to wear tight-ass Spanx that make your crotch stink so bad you have to do a quick whore bath before he heads downtown. If he was that uncomfortable with the age difference, he wouldn't be dating you. He *is* dating you. Not as a booty call or a novelty but as a boyfriend. Now chill the fuck out and stop sabotaging yourself.

DON'T TRY TO KEEP UP WITH THE JONESES, JR.

In the immortal words of every Ziggy, Garfield, and health class poster ever made, just be yourself. You don't have to feign interest in things that were interesting to you ten years ago. Nor do you have to lecture him on why he's not the first person to get into libertarianism, Woody Allen, pot growing, or The Doors. When you're in a room with a bunch of Sweet Child's friends, do your best to participate in the conversation, but stop short of enthusiastically lying about your Nickelodeon references and acting like a jaded know-it-all. Just beeee, man (exhales cloud of pot smoke). Do you think you can handle that? You can? Excellent.

LEARN HOW TO LEARN FROM EACH OTHER

You know how to compose a decent résumé and behave on a job interview. He knows where to get the cheapest anything, whether it's food, drink, clothes, or HDMI cords. You could make fun of him for sneaking flasks into bars or using packing tape as a lint brush, or you could learn all sorts of survival skills that will come in handy the next time you're unemployed or trying to cut corners. Same goes for you: He can make fun of your multiple smoke detectors or he can use them as a reminder to ask his parents to buy him one the next time he goes home. The older and younger generations do have something to learn from each other. That's why insurance companies make so many cheesy commercials about it.

FOR THE RECORD

aka Relationship Lessons from the School of Rock . . .

EVERYONE WILL SAY IT'S BECAUSE OF AGE

You are wasting your breath if you try to convince anyone otherwise. It's hurtful, it's demeaning, it's oversimplifying. However, to expect anything else is to set yourself up for disappointment. Your closest BFF might understand, but that's about all. It sucks, but that's the cross you must bear for being with such a young, tight bod whose equipment operates at max capacity. Poor you. *Wah, wah wah*. Now listen to us. We're just as bad as the people we were talking about earlier. Sorry.

YOUNG PEOPLE ARE PEOPLE, TOO

If he dumps you, it's not because he doesn't know what he wants. He knows you're not what he wants. It's just not you. If you're the one dumping him, don't assume he'll spring right back because he is young, good-looking, and his psyche is not fully formed. You can do damage for precisely that reason. That's not to say you should stay with him out of guilt. Just that you shouldn't laugh it off, even if he starts posting faux-slutty makeout pictures with someone you know is his female best friend and would make out with him only for a jokey photo op.

Sweet Child o' Mine

FUCK REGRETS

Don't focus on the age disparity such that it makes you run out and buy anti-aging creams or sign up for one of those awful dating services with a guy in a turtleneck and a woman laughing with him over yogurt. If nothing else, you had fun. Admit it. Sweet Child showed you new perspectives and allowed you to be a kid for a while. Don't let it stop you from seeing another Sweet Child or force yourself into the arms of an oldster with whom you have nothing in common. Know that you had some fun, and try to look back on it with fondness. The age discrepancy is excellent for making future boyfriends feel insecure, and that alone is worth its weight in golden Xbox controllers.

★★★ Reviews

What Critics Are Saying About Sweet Child

"We couldn't go back to his place because I was in my thirties and his 'place' was a dorm."

—Kris

"I met him when he had only been in the city for four weeks. He was wide-eyed, like a chipmunk. I had to teach him everything, including how to find an apartment."

—Shelley

"I had directed a play he was in. When he finally came to live near me, he was nineteen and I was twenty-four, and I thought I couldn't do this. The word teen *was still in there.'"*

—Cassandra

YOUR MINI PRESS KIT

Sweet Child is the guy who . . .

◆ Has the best morning-after cereal selection of any one-night-stand you've ever been on. Alpha-Bits? Lucky Charms? Hell, yes! No Fiber One or Grape-Nuts in these cupboards.

◆ Is the only reason you visit Urban Dictionary.

◆ Talks all the time about wanting a dog but can't keep a roommate around for more than a month.

◆ Kicks your ass at bar trivia and *Jeopardy!* Not because he's smarter, but because he's still fresh on everything you've forgotten since high school.

◆ Likes the same bands as you, but for all the wrong albums.

FATHER

FIGURE 9

Fig. 9a: Father Figure

- HOT: GRAY STREAKS, NOT: RECEDING HAIRLINE
- CROWS FEET, ADORABLE
- TASTEFUL V-NECK SWEATER, CORDUROY BLAZER
- WISDOM, KNOW HOW
- LEATHER BELT MATCHES LEATHER SHOES
- CLASSY OLD-FASHIONED TIMEPIECE, I.E. A WATCH
- PLEATED PANTS, YUCK
- PORTABLE CD PLAYER, STILL BUYS MUSIC
- VASECTOMY SCAR
- THE WEATHER CHANNEL SAID TO TAKE AN UMBRELLA
- SENSIBLE LOAFERS
- FRESH BAGUETTE, ARUGULA, CHEVRE, TUNISIAN OLIVE OIL, PEPTO, TYLENOL

THE MEET & GREET

Who He Is

Part senior crush, part pervy guidance counselor. A Father Figure is a guy who has some years on him, and on you, as well. At minimum five, on average ten, in rare cases twenty. Much more than that and he's not a Father Figure so much as a sexual predator, or nearsighted grandfather.

What He's All About

Father Figure is a breath of red wine, fluffy towel, and responsibility–scented air in a dating landscape of inept youngsters with poor decision-making skills and smelly sweat socks. Father Figure is a doer. A decider. He knows street names, neighborhoods, and restaurants. He has answers that other guys do not to questions such as "Where do you live?" and "Do you have a job?" He knows how to take a call during dinner without being a douche, knows how to be gracious to your parents, and can engage in an intellectual discourse on at least three different topics. A lot of folks assume girls go after Father Figures because they're flush with cash, but age and income don't necessarily climb at the same level. Experience is Father Figure's primary asset, along with perspective and wisdom. It's the kind of stuff you can't put a price on, but if you did, he'd be able to afford it or at least negotiate a more reasonable offer.

Father Figure

Turn-ons

Shoeshines, long-term investments, online banking, cute sushi waitresses, airports, sharp creases, properly inflated tires, picking up the tab, local politics, parenthetical asides, sending pictures over text (he just learned how), writing witty asides and blog commentary and thinking he's the next David Cross and/or Chuck Klosterman.

Turnoffs

Questions about his ex-wife; going somewhere with you and not getting carded; lax grammar and/or manners; Dane Cook; weddings; disorganization; recycled fads that he wasn't part of, the first time around; new bars, restaurants, and/or ideas; changes in packaging or signage; cell-phone shopping.

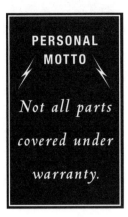

PERSONAL MOTTO

Not all parts covered under warranty.

THE HEADLINERS

For every young rocker who peaked early, whether by overexposure, underexposure, or overdose, there's another who stuck around.

Here's a look at an old-school smoothie with a voice like liquid velvet, a working-class rocker burning up the jukebox at your father and grandfather's VFW, and a Prince of Darkness turned Prince of Dementia.

BARRY WHITE

Who He Is
"The Sultan of Soul"; late Grammy Award–winning R&B singer-songwriter; founder of the Love Unlimited Orchestra, which we're assuming performs exclusively in bedrooms while wearing red velvet tuxedos.

What Makes Him Such a Father Figure
Expansive presence: If his booming voice didn't make you feel tiny, his physique would. Whereas other musicians chased the latest trend or turned political, wise Barry stayed true to his romantic roots.

Father Figure Highlights
- Stability and fidelity were the overriding themes of all his chart toppers, which include "Never, Never Gonna Give You Up," "Can't Get Enough of Your Love, Babe," and "You're the First, the Last, My Everything."
- Worked on everything from trippy disco arrangements to salad dressing commercials. He had that provider factor: No one was starving while Barry was around.
- Sired a whole bunch of children by a whole bunch of mothers—"paternity testing" was the buzz phrase at his funeral.

> "If I see a lady that attracts me to her, I walk over to her and say what I'm feeling."
>
> Barry White, BBC News, October 10, 2000

OZZY OSBOURNE

> "We've all got skeletons in our cupboards, something where you think, Oh fuck, if someone finds out about that, I'm dead."
>
> Ozzy Osbourne, *The Guardian*, May 20, 2007

Who He Is
Godfather of heavy metal, Jack and Kelly's dad, Sharon's husband, guy who used to bite the heads off bats, reality show star, dodderer.

What Makes Him Such a Father Figure
Plays the role of harried dad to perfection, despite primary child-rearing years spent on tour, shows affection to his family by engaging in foulmouthed brawls, doesn't respond well to changes in routine—once launched into a panic over a burrito.

Father Figure Highlights
- Typical Father Figure power dynamic—met wife Sharon when she was working as a receptionist for her father (Ozzy's manager at the time).
- Daughter Kelly has a tattoo in his honor and recorded a cover of Madonna's "Papa Don't Preach," two dubious daughter-father tributes, no doubt.
- The key to his continued sex life, despite his continuing birthdays? According to what he told a British mag: Viagra.

BRUCE SPRINGSTEEN

Who He Is
Born in the USA, blue-collar millionaire singer-songwriter; the only member of the E Street Band you'll ever be able to name; staple export of New Jersey; that guy who's always singing at the Super Bowl.

What Makes Him Such a Father Figure
One of a small group of rock stars who could safely perform at a nursing home without fear of persecution; has a reverence for all things vintage and storied, whether it's bandmates, guitars, or automobiles.

Father Figure Highlights
- Author of a never-ending stream of songs about the good old days (aka "Glory Days") and growing up.
- Still maintains emotional and geographical allegiance to his home state, despite having more fame and money than God (that's "Gawd" in New Jersey).
- No-nonsense fashion aesthetic: jeans, bandana, flannels, T-shirts. He looks like you imagine your father looked on the first day of high school. Maybe Mom had a point.

> "My daughter likes rap music. If there's a rapper on the radio, her and her girlfriends get in the backseat and they just lay it out; they've memorized the whole track including, like, the beeps."
>
> Bruce Springsteen,
> *Q*,
> June 23, 2009

His Regular Venues

aka Where You'll Find Him . . .

THE FARMER'S MARKET OR A HIGH-END GROCERY SHOPPE*

Father Figure doesn't go for the big once-a-month trips to the superstore like the rest of the suburbanites who drive Suburbans. He goes grocery shopping multiple times a week, like the metropolitan city dwellers and Euros. He goes there for the better selection and the higher-quality produce demanded by his sophisticated palate. After decades of eating solids, he's gotten pretty good at it. You may recoil now at the thought of monkfish terrine, but wait until Father Figure gets a hold of you. Stop in the herb section, letting the produce misters give your skin a dewy glow, and make eyes at him over the cilantro.

WORK OR A DERIVATIVE THEREOF

Father Figure is it, if you're ever going to break the DSWYE** rule and date your boss. Father Figure will start by welcoming you to the company and gradually flirt more and more and more. You will be intrigued but weirded out, but mostly just hoping to reenact the movie *Secretary* or some scene from *Mad Men*.

---

*Yeah, that's right, we said "shoppe."
**Don't shit where you eat.

Every Rose Has Its Thorn

Never before have you been so excited to go somewhere mandatory. If you don't meet Father Figure at work, you may meet him at a work mixer, conference, industry cocktail hour, or trade show. He gives you his card, but something about the way he does it lets you know that "following up" and "networking" will for once have a payoff.

A PERSONALS SITE OF LAST RESORT

You've already done some online dating. Lately the well is dry. You keep seeing the same sad headlines and the same sad headshots. You finally go to that one site, the one in all the commercials, the one your artsy friends recently parodied in a video, the one your mom has been on your ass to join since Day 1. Well, look who we have here: Father Figure. He doesn't know that the site's uncool; he just knows it's big and the most advertised one out there. He has a profile, and you respond to it. Why? Because your last boyfriend was an immature jobless lunatic five years your junior and a date with someone mature sounds lovely, even if he does crop all his pictures out where the hairline starts.

His Act

aka Ways of Working the Crowd...

TAKING IT ALL IN

Father Figure is self-confident enough to be out in the middle of the dance floor, yet he's not. He's clever enough to be at the center of the conversation, but he's probably positioned himself at the fringes, speaking only when spoken to and occasionally doling out the brilliant one-liner that gets a laugh out of everyone. Father Figure is a watcher of people. He loves to sit and study and observe, especially if it means bubbly drunk twentysomethings will toddle over to talk to the guy who looks like the beer-goggles version of George Clooney in the corner. Father Figure doesn't try to impress; he knows none of the pickup lines will work, because he went through all the hoop jumping and games years ago. If someone likes you, they like you, and they'll come over and talk to you or you'll go over and talk to them. Tricks are for kids.

BEING CONSCIENTIOUS

Right now you're asking yourself, "How is that working a crowd?" and "How is that a draw?" Simple. Whether he's selecting a brand of flatware or putting together a bedroom playlist, Father Figure puts thought into what he's doing, and nothing is sexier than a job well done. Have you ever had a deli guy so agile your perfectly prepared sandwich is wrapped and in front of you before the first half of the word "pastrami" leaves your mouth? If so, then you know what we're speaking of. Father Figure knows what movies are playing, what bands are in town, how to beat the service charges, and the best free places to park. It's like being with a concierge, but even better because he doesn't fit the typical prerequisites of being a snooty homosexual or persnickety Englishman.

CHECKING OUT YOUR BOOBAGE

Father Figure wears his advanced age like an invisibility cloak and therefore can get a little cocky sometimes. Who, me? I couldn't *possibly* be sneaking a look down your T-shirt. Look at me. I've got a suit, a sweater vest, and a nice watch. I'm drinking triple-distilled bourbon. I'm practically old enough to be your fath . . . okay, just kidding. I'm not that old. I'm actually very well preserved for my age. I'm not ancient. How old are you? Oh, wow. Ha ha! But seriously, though, you look like you're very intelligent. What was your major in college? Let me guess, something in the arts? What are you drinking? Bartender, can you get us a wine list? *Thank you.*

His Wardrobe

aka Proper & Improper Attire . . .

Fig. 9b:
For Father Figure, shoe repair is both a calling and a passion.

OLD MEETS NEW, AND IT DOESN'T GO SO WELL

Father Figure is, as your mother would say, "a sharp dresser." He more or less understands that people judge you based on appearance and that looking decent is important. He has enough years on him to have developed some semblance of personal style and enough wives and/or girlfriends to tell him what looks good and what is out of bounds. Dressing au courant is one of his only downfalls. His "hip going-out look" is frozen at whatever was popular when he was twenty-five, whether that's leather blazers or wide-leg skater pants or fuzzy woolen hippie caps indoors. It's embarrassing, but look at the bright side: If you're dating Father Figure, you're probably not going out all that often.

What He Wears

- **Seasonal items:** A decent jacket, a warm sweater, galoshes, and an umbrella. Father Figure is prepared for bad weather. Frolicking in the rain is no longer as cute as it was when he was nineteen. He has to be at work tomorrow; he can't catch a cold.
- **Work clothes:** Whether his collar is white, blue, or built into his uniform, Father Figure has a job. One that he has to be at every day and that requires him to don a specific set of clothing.

- **Aftershave:** Most guys start and stop wearing it in their early teens and don't pick up again until years and years later. You've never thought of yourself as a cologne girl, but your nostrils are telling you otherwise.
- **Quality leather goods:** As in shoes, wallets, belts. Father Figure isn't holding his pants up with a five-dollar street-vendor special or letting them fall down around his ass like an errant toddler. The shoes are one of the most expensive parts of the ensemble.
- **A watch:** Yes, they still make these. Yes, we've already told him he can just look on his cell phone.

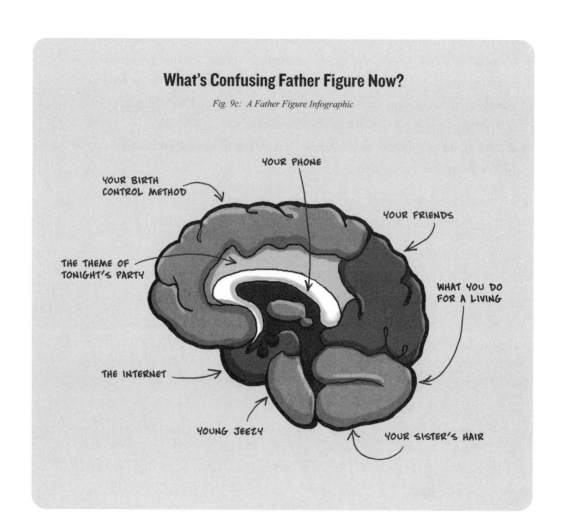

How to Get Backstage

or at the Very Least His Phone Number . . .

Fig. 9d:
Full—of issues.

ACT LIKE A LOOSE CANNON

Break all the rules, like you're in some commercial for an American-made automobile or beef jerky. Go out in your pajamas. Play five dollars' worth of Dokken in an Irish pub during lunch hour. Do ballet stretches on the pool table. Realize that this doesn't necessarily require getting sloppy drunk. Simply say and do exactly (precisely exactly) what that id part of your brain id tells you to. If you're having a hard time picturing what this is like, have a four-year-old show you.

Why It Works

Father Figure is past his act-like-a-moron years, but that doesn't mean he doesn't get a little nostalgic. You'll remind him of his heady days of limited responsibility and beer bongs. You'll also send the message that you're the kind of girl who's . . . uh . . . open. Relax. We don't mean it like it sounds. We're just saying that antics like this will show you're an independent thinker. Here is a girl who can handle dating a Father Figure. She's not going to be pressured into dating a Zac Efron clone. She's a woman, not a girl.

ACT DEMURE

We know what you're thinking, "You just told me to act skanky. What gives?" This is not a mandate to go out on the town in prairie dress and bonnet-type Latter-day Saint gear. Small changes, like reapplying lipstick in the bathroom instead of at the bar banquette while picking peppercorns out of your teeth with a business card, will go a long way here. When the jukebox is playing AC/DC, resist the urge to belt out "Back in Black" like a drunken longshoreman. When your friends are ordering shots, sip on a Seven and Seven. We're not going to lie to you. It's not as much fun. It's the price you pay for stalking the silver fox. You can go back to being a fun-loving dirtbag tomorrow.

Why It Works

The breakdown in manners and civility among today's young women is a worry to many a Father Figure. He read stories about jelly bracelets on fourth-graders signifying sexual acts and doesn't have the perspective to separate what's hype from what's real. He's secretly intrigued by this sexual aggressiveness but also turned off. It's like the closeted antigay senator. Father Figure doth protest too much. When he sees a girl acting sweet, he feels less threatened and will approach. Then when he gets to know her, he just may ask her to wear a ball gag and pee into a measuring cup. See? It all works out.

Every Rose Has Its Thorn

ISOLATE YOURSELF FROM THE OTHER ANTELOPE

We don't care if you're in a women's prison or menstrual hut, there's always a way for a girl to be alone. There are faux intestinal issues, money to be ATM'd, and crucial items at the corner store. A cunning girl will run with the pack for security but find ways to break out periodically and hunt solo. There are probably animals that do this, but we're too lazy to research, so let's just go with the lemur. Be like a wild lemur and tell your BFFs you need a moment.

Why It Works

Unlike you, Father Figure doesn't have the luxury of security in numbers. Hitting on you while you're with a group of girls is intimidating as fuck, especially when it's obvious he has a few years on you. When you're alone you're much more approachable.

PLAYLIST

Father Figure Knows Best:
Songs in the Key of Patriarchal Enchantment

1. **"Girl, You'll Be a Woman Soon"—Neil Diamond, 1967, Metronome**
   Neil says, "Soon, you'll need a man," to which we say, "Sure, but does it have to be such an old one?"

2. **"To All the Girls I've Loved Before"—Julio Iglesias & Willie Nelson, 1984, CBS**
   Two seasoned Casanovas manage to make years of slutting around with groupies sound like the inside of a Hallmark card.

3. **"She's Always a Woman"—Billy Joel, 1977, Columbia**
   Billy Joel loves you, kiddo, even though he's convinced you college chicks are all bipolar.

4. **"Just Like a Woman"—Bob Dylan, 1966, Columbia**
   Bob Dylan wants to touch that very special part of you that's both courageous and vulnerable. Surprise! It's your boobs.

5. **"Three Times a Lady"—The Commodores, 1978, Motown**
   Lionel and the boys know that some girls tire of twee indie ballads that tiptoe around the edges of sentimentality. They want to be romanced. *Hard.*

POP QUIZ

Do You Have Your Father Figured? A Day in the Life

Fill in the blanks and find out if your guy is the latest jam or a golden oldie.
In the morning, he . . .

1. Gets out of bed and:
   a. Shuffles off to bathroom. Urinates.
   b. Turns off white-noise machine. Removes bite guard.

2. Eats a breakfast of:
   a. Coffee, yogurt, and granola.
   b. Raisin Bran, the local news, and a multivitamin.

3. Stops for gas and throws _____ on the counter as an impulse purchase.
   a. A fancy iced tea.
   b. A roll of Tums.

4. At work, engages in a morning gripe session about:
   a. How lame MTV is now.
   b. His roofing contractors.

5. Works a bit, then goofs off by:
   a. Watching episodes of The Office.
   b. Playing Sudoku.

6. Leaves work and:
   a. Goes to happy hour.
   b. Goes to happy hour and calls in sick the following morning.

7. Comes home, sorts the mail, and:
   a. Talks to his roommate.
   b. Talks to himself.

8. Logs on to his dating profile and:
   a. Messages several girls who look interesting.
   b. Messages everyone, including the site administrator and the model in the stock photo.

9. Before going to bed, he:
   a. Looks at TV.
   b. Looks at the thermostat.

10. Has insomnia and:
    a. Watches TV.
    b. Checks his 401(k) balance.

(continued)

SCORING

MOSTLY A'S = LATEST JAM
He's what's on everyone's playlist. Will he be headlining at a wedding reception five years from now? Perhaps even your own? It's too early to tell.

MOSTLY B'S = GOLDEN OLDIE
You're listening to 100.8 O-L-D, the only station for Father Figures and the women who love them. Caller, are you there? Caller?

IF YOU DECIDE TO BOOK HIM FOR ONE NIGHT ONLY

aka the Ins and Outs of Being Friends with Benefits . . .

 *The Pros*

YOU WILL FEEL GREAT ABOUT YOUR BODY

There are some of you who love your body and that's just fab. However, for a lot of you, it's more complicated. But fear no more, because your naked bod is the

 Every Rose Has Its Thorn

best three-dimensional representation of a woman Father Figure has seen in a long, long while. He will praise you and compliment you and make you feel like the gorgeous babe you should already believe you are. Plus, next to his moobs and spindly calves, you will realize that everyone has flaws and it's downhill from here. Enjoy the upper hand while you've got it.

LOCATION, LOCATION, LOCATION

Father Figure's place is always more or less ready for a rendezvous. A few dirty dishes, a smattering of razor stubble on the sink. Otherwise, it's all there: clean bed, soap, hand towel, cold beverages. Father Figure can host a fling—even a work-night fling—on very short notice. Once you slept over and were able to snag a shirt his teen daughter had left there during one of her weekend visits. A little creepy, but at least you were able to look fresh for your client meeting the next morning.

NO GIMP JACKET REQUIRED

There's built-in kink by simple virtue of his being older. Who needs leather restraints and hundred-dollar vibrators shaped like small mammals when you can slip into all these roles: Lolita, ingénue, wayward schoolgirl, virgin (Ha!). They're not doing anything for the women's movement, but what's more liberating than indulging sick desires? Fantasies know no politics, and your NOW membership is still current. Call him Daddy if that's what you're into. Unless he wants you to put on frilly socks and turn on *Blue's Clues* while you screw, there's no need to worry.

The Cons

STRUCTURAL INTEGRITY

Penises are like airplanes; most problems occur during takeoff (adolescence: premature ejaculation) and landing (middle age: erectile dysfunction). Though no one gets killed by a nonfunctioning penis, so perhaps this is too bleak a metaphor. What we're trying to say is that some Father Figures will have issues with performing. It's not an automatic given that everything will be cool in that department. With a boyfriend, you can work with this; with a booty call, it's more unfortunate. This may be the one time he's in town or you have a break from your ridiculous job and your only chance to get laid for the next month, and all you've got is a clit pacing around the bedroom and a snoring hairy Kenny Rogers double beside you. The upside is that Father Figures are of an age where it's not awkward to ask them to go on Viagra and then, whooo boy, look out. Get yourself some Motrin and a doughnut pillow.

HEY! NOT SO EAGER WITH THE BEAVER!

Father Figure doesn't know when to leave well enough alone. He assumes since you're young that means you're a sex kitten who wants to boink all night. Even worse, he assumes *you* assume he has to want to boink all night. He fucks like he's got something to prove, finishing up and then pawing at you before the condom's even off from the first time. Sure, a porno three-times-in-a-row romp might be fun, but not *every time*. He already cared enough to get you off, which puts him ahead of a lot of the younger guys. Greed isn't sexy. You need a fuck

Every Rose Has Its Thorn

friend who can treat you like a friend, not like a traveling porn star or someone who's on a conjugal visit in prison.

LIMITED HOURS

Father Figure has a demanding job, an attribute that would be appealing were he a boyfriend, but he's not. A warm bed and the ability to work the night shift are the only requirements. Father Figure has travel plans, conferences, and big important clients. There may also be offspring to think about, and meetings with his divorce lawyer. The older you are, the more responsibilities you have and the less able you are to drop everything and fuck like a factory-farm mink, despite what they'd lead you to believe on Spanish soap operas.

IF YOU DECIDE TO MAKE HIM THE HOUSE BAND

aka from Groupie to Girlfriend and Beyond . . .

 *The Pros*

MATURE AND CONSIDERATE: WHAT A CONCEPT!

Father Figure is not big on games, petty fights, drama, or anything frequently mentioned in the lyrics of Mary J. Blige songs. He returns calls promptly and holds doors as much as he holds his tongue. He doesn't throw a tantrum if you have male friends, and will always grab your luggage off the carousel, even if you're fighting at the airport. If issues arise, his first instinct is to talk it out. There's no storming off and leaving you in parking lots like there was in high school and college. For this reason the damaged part of your psyche might find him really, really boring.

SEE YOU AT THE MALT SHOP

Father Figure's romantic streak is strong. It's not pathetic romantic, like a marigold plucked from the neighbor's yard presented in a Aquafina bottle, nor is it dork romantic, like the *Dark Towers* boxed set you got from your college boyfriend (you've never seen or even mentioned the show). It's a combination of traditional—roses, wine, crème brûlée, perfume—and thoughtful—fixing the squeak in your bedframe, and bathroom-mirror Post-it notes. He makes things like picnics and carriage rides and rowboats sound like realistic options. You've even started researching retreats in the Catskills.

COUCH POTATO'S BEST FRIEND

Father Figure is no slouch. He enjoys going out to dinner and the movies, but he excels at staying home. His couch is expansive; there are no roommates wandering around. It's a comfortable place to hang out. Father Figure has a big TV and home theater system, but unlike his younger peers, they don't have to be unhooked from the gaming system or laptop. Lying in his arms on the La-Z-Boy sectional, you realize that Father Figure's house is nicer than your own, and you plan on enjoying the privileges of membership as much as possible.

The Cons

CONSTANT CONDESCENSION

Go ahead, Father Figure. Say it. Say "When I was your age . . ." one more time. See if you don't wind up with a rearranged soft palate. Father Figure uses his age as a bargaining tool, a decision finalizer, an anger justifier, and a guilt inducer. Multifunctional, all-purpose, ready to whip out on any occasion. It's an emotional Swiss Army knife. You realize there is a lot to learn from his experience. However, you don't see how it's germane to the great peanut debate: creamy or crunchy. (P.S. The right answer is always crunchy.) You've told Father Figure how much it bothers you when he pulls this crap, but he cannot stop. It's an automatic behavior by this point.

SINGLE FOR A REASON

We're not big on "All the good ones are taken!" or "Deep-throat a rifle if you haven't found a husband by the age of thirty-five!" However, we all know that the funnel narrows. Because it narrows, there's a great chance you're going to run into some psychos as the age chart approaches the upper echelons. Some (though obviously not all) Father Figures are adept at creating the illusion of sanity for the first few months, a sort of biological adaptation to ensure their survival, along with watching *The OC* for conversational topics and buying expensive vintage T-shirts from the museum design shop. *"Look at me! I'm young! I'm hip! I'm opened-minded!"* Yes, but you jerk back on the seat of the person in front of you for leverage when getting up on airplanes, and your breath tastes like coffee brewed in a corpse. These traits are undesirable at any age, but at twenty-five at least there's the thin hope that someone will grow out of it.

FRIEND WEIRDNESS

Father Figure is shy about meeting your friends. He won't outright say it. Something will always come up until it gets to be like a bad *Brady Bunch* episode where he fakes a head cold or phones in a bomb threat to the local Olive Garden

where you're about to make the big introduction. To be fair, you don't want to hang out with Father Figure's friends, either. You've also been avoiding it. Neither of you wants to be judged, but the funny thing is, the more you avoid friends, the more they'll be filling in the gaps and making up stories. Then it gets even weirder, and the federal marshals get called in because someone's the subject of elder abuse or being taken as a child bride.

HOW TO END IT HARMONIOUSLY

WITH AN EMPTY BUCKET

An people have something they want to do in their lifetime, even if that thing is to do nothing. Until now, you've been subtle about your pre-grave to-do list. No use scaring anyone off. Now's the time to lay it all out there. Tell him what you want to do and when, and what you will not compromise on. Such a show of honesty and candor will force most Father Figures to figure out what they want. Or do they need another twenty years to think about it? What's the rush? Odds are Father Figure either can't or doesn't want to hang, and it won't be long before he starts hobbling along.

WITH A REDUCED BENEFITS PACKAGE

Father Figure will be bummed (very bummed) when you have the breakup talk. Expect him to be offended when you drunk-text him, weeks later, asking him to come over and play dirty-word Scrabble. Wait another few weeks and try again. He'll pick up. Hot ass like you doesn't come around often, and it's certainly more exciting than the women he's meeting in his book club. He's willing to swallow his pride in order to get laid once in a while. A friend-with-benefits is one of the few parts of the modern sexual landscape that he's able to get excited about and that will make him sound "on trend" to his next conquest.

WITH A QUESTIONING OF AUTHORITY

Along with chivalry and good manners comes complacency. You need to feel what it's like to make your own choices, to challenge his decisions instead of simpering and kowtowing like a Hollywood agent or pharmacist. Because guess what? *He's not that cool.* He was just born before you. Once he knows you know that, the relationship is on dangerous ground. The emperor has no mojo, just a middle-management job and nine out of ten punches on his Subway club card. Accept it, make it known, and the battle is 90 percent over.

HOW TO KEEP MAKING SWEET MUSIC TOGETHER

GIVE CREDIT TO THE GUY WHO HAS THE BEST CREDIT
In the beginning you *ooh*ed and *ahh*ed over Father Figure's every little capability and achievement. Now, like an eight-year-old who's just starting to recognize that his dad isn't the coolest, strongest, or fastest dad in the whole universe, you're undergoing a period of crippling disillusionment. Must he eat the same tuna fish sandwich for lunch every day? Make the same tired-ass puns? Give you a lecture about discretion every time you say a cuss word on your work e-mail? The short answer is yes. This is who he is, and if you want to be with him, you have to embrace that aspect. Father Figure's solidity, experience, and responsibility are a big part of the reason why you're with him. Don't lose that by rebelling for no real purpose.

DIMENSIONALITY ISN'T A DEALBREAKER
You love a rich and storied past, but Father Figure stretches that tolerance. Whether it's a host of ex-wives, drunken revelations of bisexual encounters, colonoscopy reminder stickers on the fridge, or children's toys in the bedroom in which you fuck, you're just not quite ready for the reality of it all. However, fast-forward twenty years. Actually, make that ten. You will have been through multiple jobs, multiple apartments, and multiple roommates, and possibly multiple husbands. Would you want a man judging you for this? Of course not. You'd

Father Figure

say, "What I've been through is what I am," and you should think the same of Father Figure.

GET YOUR OWN YARDSTICK

You may not have as much experience with life, jobs, nuptials, putting money into (as opposed to taking money out of) a bank account. Before you get all down on yourself, remember that Father Figure has had a head start. You can't judge yourself by his achievements any more than you can a toddler for not enunciating. We all go through life at our own pace, and while it's okay to covet Father Figure's wise observations and cool ironic distance in the face of disturbing events as well his really expensive Danish modern furniture, it's not okay to get down on yourself for not yet having achieved something similar. It's also not cool to act resentful or force him to share the wealth. Yeah, if you've got a crap copy-editing job and he wants to pay for more of the dinners, fine, but it should by no means be expected. You'll get there, we swear. If not, then some version of There that's even cooler than what he has right now.

 Every Rose Has Its Thorn

FOR THE RECORD

aka Relationship Lessons from the School of Rock . . .

EVERYONE WILL SAY IT'S BECAUSE OF AGE

Just like Sweet Child, now and forever, the age difference will be the go-to explanation for your breakup. *Always.* "You need someone fun!" "You need someone your own age." "He was just a playboy, the kind that never grows up." You can fight the assumptions, or you can drink heavily and trust in the knowledge that those who matter know the real deal. All it takes to get through a breakup or even just run-of-the-mill couple's fights with Father Figure is the understanding of one person.

BARTLETT'S BOOK IS FULL OF LIARS

With age comes wisdom. Experience is the best teacher. A wrinkled ball in time saves nine. There are all sorts of assumptions that go along with getting old, and your relationship with Father Figure has proven that a lot of them are true. However, a lot of them are rot. There are May-December relationships where the male has all the power, and there are ones where he is at the complete mercy of his young consort. *What do you mean, they're out of chocolate soy milk? Did you drive to the place across town?* Father Figure is a person, not an archetype or a symbol. He has inconsistencies and natural variations. Like the garment care label says, these are not necessarily indicative of flaws.

Father Figure

UNKNOWNS CAN BE CONQUERED

You were scared at first, but then you realized he puts his out-of-date Lee jeans on one leg at a time like anyone else. Guys are guys; the differences are mostly just details. What was once scary is now mundane. The exotic is unraveled. You can now go on to date foreign guys, girls, people who don't share your political affiliation, flip-flop wearers, and those who still carry pencils. You will feel less strange about pairing up with someone who isn't a precise match for you and more confident that it can work out. This can have excellent consequences, as it opens up your dating pool. *All in!*

Every Rose Has Its Thorn

★★★ Reviews

What Critics Are Saying About Father Figure

"He was classy. He was confident. He dressed like my dad, if my dad were classy and confident. He slept naked and wore a Hugh Hefner robe in the a.m. He had investments almost as old as I was."

—Willa

"I had dated guys who didn't have jobs for a very, very long time, so Tom was really awesome. I was talking to my ex and I was like, 'You have to get a job, because having a job is totally going to get you a girl. It's awesome!'"

—Becca

"Go for it. But remember that if he's ten years older than you and acts five years younger, he ain't ever growing up."

—Shirley

YOUR MINI PRESS KIT

Father Figure is the guy who . . .

✦ Can school you on complicated investment strategies but keeps sending you viruses on Facebook.

✦ Arrives at your "40s Party" in period clothes with a martini shaker instead of malt liquor and an Adidas sweatsuit.

✦ Has at least one old-school STD in his past. You know it's wrong to say, but the notion of his having "The Clap" is kinda cute.

✦ Is a bit like a Gremlin in that he gets really cranky if you keep him up past midnight.

✦ Owns a library card and actually uses it.

✦ Has lots of baggage but really nice luggage.

MR.

ROBOTO

10

Fig. 10a: Mr. Roboto

- WIKIPEDIA ENTRY DEVELOPMENT CENTER
- DORKY HAIRCUT (HASN'T CHANGED SINCE ELEMENTARY SCHOOL)
- UNIBROW
- ILL-FITTING HOODIE
- HIGH CAPACITY THUMB DRIVE
- DRAGONCON T-SHIRT SIGNED BY PANELISTS
- LAPTOP BAG
- UTILITY BELT
- IMPORTED INDECIPHERABLE JAPANESE DIGITAL WATCH
- CAMERA FOR OBSESSIVE DOCUMENTATION
- HIDEOUS SHORTS
- BETA "TESTERS ONLY" PORTABLE GAMING SYSTEM
- BINARY CODE TATTOO
- BLACK SOCKS

THE MEET & GREET

Who He Is

A nerd. The original tried-and-true socially awkward version, before it was cool to go around buying Members Only reissues at Urban Outfitters and saying, "I was such a dork." The one who contacts you on Facebook, but you don't remember him going to your high school. Weird Al before he got a record deal. The guy you were about to hit on before you started to wonder whether you had seen him in a documentary about guys who live with Japanese love dolls.

What He's All About

Genius intellectually. Idiot emotionally. Scores in the 99.9th percentile on standardized tests but hasn't scored nearly so well with women. Will spend hours researching old experimental jazz musicians, yet shops for new clothes once every ten years because he's "so busy." Has obscure health issues and orthopedic shoes but can bring your computer back from the brink of extinction. Is terrible at first in bed but responds incredibly well after a little bit of training. Mr. Roboto loves to debate but hurts people's feelings sometimes because he doesn't know when to back down. He has a hard time expressing himself. Whenever he does, it always comes off stilted and weird. Lucky for him, "weird" is what's in now.

> **PERSONAL MOTTO**
>
> To thine own avatar be true.

Turn-ons

Seeing your iPod on the first date, checking the weather forecast, correcting people, friendships based on obscure niche interests, Mucinex, musty bookstores, overclocking his processor, forming deep online relationships with total strangers.

Turnoffs

The beach, bars where sports are played, empathy, small talk, magazines, "greatest hits" compilations, girls who watch the wrong *Star Trek,* high school reunions, being asked to refrain from fact-checking on his iPhone.

THE HEADLINERS

Many nerdy guys play rock 'n' roll. A select few are able to make a brand out of it. Some do it through sheer persistence, like the kid who was never invited but always managed to show up at every high school party. Others shoot to fame after starting out as a joke (see also William Hung), then being taken seriously once they record a multiplatinum album.

To get this party started, here's an all-star lineup of Mr. Robotos past and present, from a nearsighted 1950s icon to a pale Scotsman with a canary falsetto to a prog rock demigod.

 **Every Rose Has Its Thorn**

BUDDY HOLLY

Who He Is
Rockabilly saint. Once rejected by the army for lack of physical fitness. Did behind-the-scenes AV Club–type work for everyone from Waylon Jennings to Elvis.

What Makes Him Such a Mr. Roboto
Trademark horn-rims launched a nerdy-on-purpose eyewear trend that's spanned well over half a century. Always wore a suit to perform in. Music geek purist even Eddie Vedder would be proud of. Wrote and produced almost all of his own material.

> "It might pick back up, but I really doubt it."
>
> Buddy Holly on whether rock music would last, 1957 radio interview with Red Robinson

Mr. Roboto Highlights
- Always a runner-up, never a Romeo; hit single "Peggy Sue" was *not* about a girl he was romancing but rather his drummer's girlfriend.
- First date with wife was lunch at a Howard Johnson's. Nice choice of venue, Bud.
- Mr. Roboto band of brothers Weezer paid homage to him in a song bearing his name. The video, made in the '90s, is a parody of a show made in the '70s, which is about teens in the '50s. *Meta!*

DAVID BYRNE

Who He Is
Chief head of the Talking Heads; preternaturally talented, critically and commercially successful solo artist; sufferer of the sexiest case of Crazy Eye this side of Boston.

What Makes Him Such a Mr. Roboto
Nerds make other nerds, and over the years Mr. Byrne has amassed four Internets' worth of nerd-on-nerd validation. If that's not enough, there's also his Wahl clipper guard #4 haircut, pencil neck, and thick eyebrows, as well as side careers as PowerPoint artist in residence and opera/ballet composer.

> **Mr. Roboto Highlights**
> - Has a hard time understanding the opposite sex. Typical song lyric: "The women are talking / We do not understand," from "Women vs. Men (Bolero)."
> - Former bandmates have implied that his relationships fail because he is first and foremost concerned about his artistic legacy. Then nerds wonder why they can't get laid.
> - Likes women with big right brains. Occupations of last three girlfriends: costume designer, art curator, photographer.

"I saw these Japanese kids dancing in the park in Tokyo, these kind of rockabilly dancers, and then there were these kind of space cadet kids that had a completely different set of movements. I videotaped a bunch of them, and that's where I got that."

David Byrne on his unique dance style, *Pitchfork*, July 17, 2006

Every Rose Has Its Thorn

GEDDY LEE

Who He Is
Lead vocalist and bassist for Canadian rock outfit Rush; ponytail custodian; prophesier/soothsayer/scariest person on earth to anyone under the influence of marijuana.

What Makes Him Such a Mr. Roboto
Has been in show business for over three decades and yet still sports granny glasses, Yanni hair, and a soul patch. Sings about everything from social issues to sci-fi to libertarianism but rarely, if ever, girls.

> **Mr. Roboto Highlights**
> - Bio on official Rush website contains extensive gear list detailing bass and amp specs but no mention of wife, family, or anything relating to being a human.
> - Once referred to women at Rush concerts as "geddycorns," alluding to the fact that they were "mythical and seldom seen."
> - Made cameo appearance on *The Colbert Report*. Nerd fan base got irate when show cut to commercial mid-song.

"I was a quiet nerd . . . I remember seeing Cream when they came around— nobody wanted to go with me."

Geddy Lee,
Heeb,
April 1, 2009

His Regular Venues
aka Where You'll Find Him . . .

FIRST IN LINE
For Mr. Roboto, punctuality is close to godliness. Anywhere there's a movie premiere, software release, or debut of a game system or cell phone, you'll be sure to find him. He's not so over-the-top as to be the guy with the rainbow wig and the cardboard sign. He'll be standing outside the Apple store as if that's what he always does at four a.m. on a Tuesday, not talking to anybody and pretending to be totally *not* excited. (P.S. He's ecstatic.)

IN A VENUE THAT'S NOT A VENUE
Mr. Robotos love hearing music in places where music is not usually expected: a basement, a back room, a floating art boat made out of recycled materials. Said venue usually smells like someone's been putting out cigarettes in his armpits, but that's not the point. It's authentic, and that's what matters. This way, he can get up close with the musicians, steal their set lists off the stage, take snapshots of their equipment, and make them uncomfortable by asking them if they want to get together and jam later.

Every Rose Has Its Thorn

A DATING SITE

Sounds odd, but when you think about Mr. Roboto's lack of social skills and lack of participation in the social mainstream, it makes perfect sense. And unlike a party with a bunch of guys who dress better and charm better, here's a place where he has an edge. He knows how to Photoshop, how to game the system to get his profile listed in the first page of results, how to get free credits, and how to tell when his e-mails are being read and at what time. If he can keep that knowledge to himself and refrain from sounding like a stalker, he might get somewhere.

His Act

aka Ways of Working the Crowd . . .

DOCUMENTING HIMSELF AND EVERYONE AROUND HIM

Be it a Chinese New Year parade or corpse flower exhibit, Mr. Roboto will be capturing the event on every available medium, then using all sorts of plug-ins and homemade hacks to post the information using multiple ways and means. Case in point, he took so many photos of shirtless women at the gay pride parade that he almost got beat up by a group of irate lesbians. What they don't realize is that those shots make up about twenty out of twenty thousand. Mr. Roboto also has the same number of photos of garbage, street signs, and coincidentally, men's privates. His rabid attention to detail and his quest for complete coverage bring him into contact with many available females but close conversation with none.

CLUSTERING AROUND OTHER MR. ROBOTOS

How is it that a *Star Trek* convention in a tiny Podunk town can bring out more people than a visit from the president? Simple. Mr. Robotos are like bacteria: Under the right conditions, they will spread and flourish in number. They do it for protection. They do it for enjoyment. Mostly, they do it because they don't know any other way not to. The downside of this is that it can make them incredibly difficult to approach. The upside is that, at a crowded party, you can do a quick scan of the room and find the cutest guy in the colony that most closely matches your interest. Look, see? There's the science guys over there by the kitchen, and the bike modders over by the Tostitos and salsa, and the programmers over by the firepit. If only regular guys could self-organize like this. They're a potpourri. Mr. Robotos are more efficient and manageable.

BEING HARD TO TALK TO

Mr. Roboto has a special knack for making himself unavailable for contact by girls. If he's not engaging in either of the above activities, he's deep in conversation with an extremely attractive female friend who looks like a girlfriend (who's rejected him on three separate occasions, so clearly she's not) or eating a really unappealing, odor-emitting foodstuff. Oddly enough, in the back of his mind, in his secret heart of hearts, he's there to meet a girl. To get him to understand the counterproductive nature of the aforementioned behaviors is, unfortunately, outside his scope of understanding. Why shouldn't he hang out with this hot girl? She's nice. Why shouldn't he eat falafel with extra tahini and garlic? He's hungry. He's not there to "play games" unless it's Battleship or The Settlers of Catan.

His Wardrobe

aka Proper & Improper Attire...

THE ACCIDENTAL HIPSTER

Mr. Roboto's style looks trendy but it hasn't changed since high school. It's just been made mass market. In fact, the first time you see him, you might write off Mr. Roboto as another disaffected, coke-addled party boy who spends his time jacking off to back issues of *Nylon*. Oh, how wrong. Try a guy who wears out-of-date frames because he's been wearing them so long he doesn't even notice them anymore. They're part of his face now. Same goes for his ill-fitting jeans and mismatched socks. If he looked in the mirror instead of reading books on how they're made, this wouldn't be a problem.

Fig. 10b: His imported Japanese digital performs twelve hundred functions. Telling time is not one of them.

What He Wears

- T-shirts: from programming and gamer conventions, ones emblazoned with science jokes that take fifteen minutes to explain and are never, ever humorous.
- Same hairstyle he's had since his first haircut. Luckily, it's back in style now.
- Wears the same shoe from the same company every day until they wear out. When the company goes out of business, will hit eBay to keep the dream going.

Mr. Roboto

- Man bag with fifty books, two high-capacity flash drives, allergy medicine, a gross of pencils.
- Eau de Mr. Roboto: a proprietary blend of shaving cream, rainy library, old books, and repressed sexual energy.

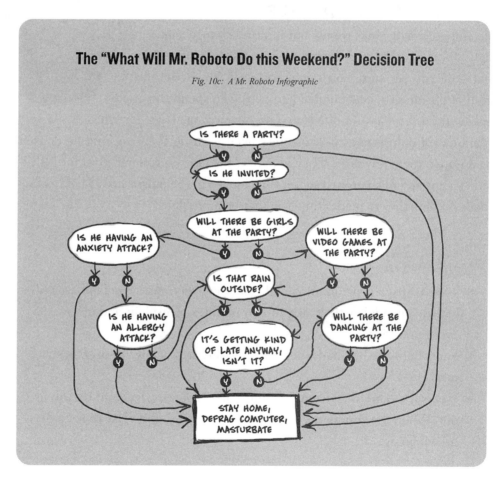

How to Get Backstage
or at the Very Least His Phone Number . . .

CORRECT HIM ON SOMETHING
"Oh hi, I came across your blog on antique theremin repair and I couldn't help but notice that your technique is all wrong . . ." Movie and book themes, trivia, and quotations are also hot topics. If it's part of a trilogy, that's even more of a bonus. Show him how much you know about what he thinks he knows. It's doubtful he'll agree with you, but at least you'll get a discussion going.

Fig. 10d: Mr. Roboto's avatar—a portrait in unchecked nerdery.

Why It Works
This brings together three things Mr. Roboto can't get enough of: debating, niche nerd topics, and the opportunity to talk to a cute girl about both of the above. Correcting him shows you have at least some knowledge of his interest, which he'll find sexy. Then you can get him interested in your interest, and before long you'll be doing interesting things and making interesting babies together (unless that's an interest that doesn't interest you at all).

CREATE AN ALTER EGO
You can do it literally, by becoming an elf princess or a violent futuristic gunslinger, or you can do it in a less fanciful way, by hanging around a couple of political, science, or music sites and becoming an active, engaged commenter. Note that the latter isn't someone who makes multiple comments on one day

Mr. Roboto

concerning one issue. Not only does it take a daily commitment, you have to develop your own brand and style. You have to mix the topical with the personal. You'll know you're doing it right when you don't comment for a couple of days and the other commenters put up posts like, "Monkey1976, wHere R u??"

Why It Works

Like most of us, Mr. Roboto feels more comfortable in a chat room than he does at a cocktail party. Unlike most of us, Mr. Roboto actually makes friends this way, as in real, live people who meet for Risk tournaments and coffee. You can be one of those people. Just be sure to be safe about it. Do some Google checking on some of his social networking profiles. He's only got about twenty, so it shouldn't be a problem.

BE A REVERSE MAGPIE

He's low-pro in social settings to the point where people forget he's a member of your party. Although well regarded and well liked, he often gets left off lists and e-mail invitations. If you want some hot nerd love, you're going to have to train yourself to look for the person who doesn't want to be looked at. Yes to quiet frumpy dude in corner; no to clever cute-hair chatterbox.

Why It Works

Mr. Roboto is passive (see also: scared, chickenshit, overthinks to the point of comic tragedy). However, if you notice him, even with a gesture as small as a smile and some eye contact, you're in there like corrective lenswear. He'll want

you and only you. No need to worry about holding on to his attention or having a foolproof opener.

PLAYLIST

Nerd Pop Pity Party: Songs Mr. Roboto Will Listen to When Troubled by Affairs of the Heart

1. **"You Got Lucky"—Tom Petty & The Heartbreakers, 1982, Backstreet**
   For every unfortunate-looking nice guy who's been tossed aside for someone more stereotypically good-looking.
2. **"Undone—The Sweater Song"—Weezer, 1994, DGC**
   Knitting needles meet nerd catharsis and the greatest of all Mr. Roboto fears: public nudity.
3. **"I Don't Want to Get Over You"—The Magnetic Fields, 1999, Merge**
   This is what he plays when he sees those Facebook pictures of you whooping it up with your new boyfriend.
4. **"Sorry"—Nerf Herder, 1996, My Records/Arista Records**
   This is what he plays when he sees those pictures again, two hours later and six beers drunker.
5. **"One More Minute"—Weird Al, 1985, Scotti Brothers**
   The official anthem of the anger phase as it inches toward acceptance. Dead-on doo-wop and lyrics so hyperbolic he can't help chuckling.

POP QUIZ

Finding Your Ideal Mr. Roboto

As we nerverts know, Mr. Robotos come in all types, shapes, and forms. Which nerdy subset gets *you* hot under the buttoned-all-the-way-up collar?

1. You'll meet him at a:
   a. Party he's throwing. Tons of people are there.
   b. Party he's throwing. Hardly anyone showed up, but he spends half the night talking about how it's too crowded.
   c. Party he wasn't invited to. He just wandered in.

2. He'll be wearing:
   a. A Ben Sherman shirt and Penguin windbreaker.
   b. A thrift store sweater, old Levis resurrected from high school (they fit better now).
   c. Pants. Maybe.

3. He'll complete the look with:
   a. Ray-Ban Wayfarers, vintage Japanese Nikes.
   b. A pocketful of guitar picks, a paper bracelet from a show.
   c. A rubber band around his wrist and a scratch-off Lotto card.

4. His friends are all:
   a. DJs, band managers, models (think less haute couture and more shot girl).
   b. Mostly people he shares a hobby with, a couple of randoms from high school.
   c. People he met earlier that day or the day before.

5. On your first date you'll go:
   a. To an exquisitely dilapidated Italian restaurant, then a sold-out show.
   b. For four-dollar dumplings, then some dubiously impressive local landmark.
   c. To "dinner," which turns out to be fending off sexual advances on his futon.

6. For your six-month anniversary he'll buy you:
   a. A gold necklace with angel wings.
   b. A gold necklace with a hedgehog pendant.
   c. A gold necklace held together by a safety pin (possibly stolen?).

7. The first time you get in a tussle it will be over:
   a. The hot babe in an American Apparel ad.
   b. His stifled laughs and snarky smirks. It's your best friend's book reading. Come on.
   c. Something disturbing you found on his hard drive.

8. His dream girls:
   a. Amelie, Audrey, Angelina
   b. Patti Smith, Patty Hearst, Peppermint Patty
   c. Dakota Fanning, an unspecified QVC host, Jenna Jameson

9. If you ever break up, it's probably going to be because:
   a. He talks too much.
   b. He doesn't talk enough.
   c. He talks to himself, and often it's in a scream or whisper.

SCORING

MOSTLY A'S = FASHION NERD
He's not a nerd. He's a regular-guy-in-nerd-clothing. Which has its advantages. He won't bore you to death with flame war recaps and can take care of himself when left to his own devices. However, if you're the one spinning yarns about your giant Steampunk seagull that's going to be exhibited at Burning Man, there may be a problem. That is, assuming he didn't already book when he found out those adorable glasses you wear are actually sporting a pretty serious prescription.

MOSTLY B'S = NERD'S NERD
Look up *nerd* in the dictionary (oh, excuse us, *Wiktionary*), and this guy is in the definition. In fact, The *Musical Influences: 1983–1985* section just isn't doing him justice. Let's not even *discuss* the resolution of the photo. This kind of attention to detail is what makes you love him. It's also what makes you fantasize about breaking it off and taking up with a gorgeous but dumb-as-a-bag-of-frozen-peas humanities major.

MOSTLY C'S = NON-NERD OTHER
Oooh, girl. You hit the jackpot of wackpots. Keep your wits about you, and watch for newspaper hoarding and visible body lice. Charles Manson was once a quirky babe magnet with a beard and a guitar.

IF YOU DECIDE TO BOOK HIM FOR ONE NIGHT ONLY

aka the Ins and Outs of Being Friends with Benefits...

 *The Pros*

HE'S ENTHUSIASTIC

If there were ever a "Sex with You" convention, Mr. Roboto would be camping out in the sleet and hail for tickets. He has absolutely *nothing* better to do than come when you call because Mr. Roboto has been waiting all his life to be used like a common floozy. He has fantasized about it since he was a wee teen and thus will be your biggest bedroom fanboy.

HE WANTS TO EXCEL

Mr. Roboto will apply the same level of dedication and commitment that helped him build an award-winning Sims empire to making you orgasm. Once he's mastered that, he'll move on to multiple orgasms, something you never thought possible, given your lack of focus and persnickety vagina. To Mr. Roboto, this is a quest, like rare comic book collecting, and he wants to be the guy holding the issue of *The Watchmen*. You're mostly indifferent toward a lot of his endeavors, but this is one you can really get behind.

HE'S INCAPABLE OF BEING SHOCKED
You're having wild drunk sex and then—*bam*—you say/do/request something totally bizarre and out of character. But like a seamless handoff of the baton at the 1996 Montreal Olympic games, Mr. Roboto plays right along and actually seems to like it. You worry that he's a bit worldly, but after getting to know him better, you realize that just because he's familiar with it and has read about it and watched it on YouTube doesn't mean he's actually experienced it. It's like the five-year-old who has read the encyclopedia and is getting to apply his knowledge for the first time.

The Cons

HE WILL MAKE YOU FEEL GUILTY
Mr. Roboto always says he's fine with a casual arrangement, but his fumbling stares and awkward texts say otherwise. Every time you confront him about his latest *Scientific American* link referencing the importance of one-on-one pair bonding in the fruit bat community, he swears up and down that he has no hard feelings, it's just a coincidence, and you're being paranoid.

Mr. Roboto

HE'S A CONTROVERSIAL CHOICE OF PARTNER

It can be embarrassing to introduce him to your friends, many of whom are in couples and rely on stories of your hot fuck buddies to warm their loins vicariously. You normally talk him up, because he is good in bed. It's only when you take him out in public that you notice everything you first saw when you met him: the postnasal drip, the black socks with shorts, the unibrow, the knock-knock-joke telling. It seems hard to justify, like you're the owner of a tattoo shop and your latest hire has a fear of needles.

HE DOESN'T EXERCISE COMMON SENSE

How many ways does Mr. Roboto kill the mood? There aren't enough stars in Carl Sagan's galaxy: correcting the spelling in your dirty texts, accidentally inviting friends over to the apartment to check out the view from your rooftop when you were leading him home to make out, taking everything literally—when you tell him you want to take him upstairs (wink, wink) to see your record collection, *he actually asks to see your record collection*. He's absorbed in liner notes for the next ninety minutes and he chides you for not being more diligent with your dust jackets.

IF YOU DECIDE TO MAKE HIM THE HOUSE BAND

aka from Groupie to Girlfriend and Beyond...

 *The Pros*

HE'S LOYAL BY DEFAULT

Out of all our guys, Mr. Roboto is just about the last guy you'd worry about cheating. For all his brilliance, he also maintains a chronic blind spot. He gets so absorbed in what he's doing and who he's with that he completely fails to notice other people. He'll go to a hot party and be able to tell you the sound system specs and the history of the venue (it once belonged to the Freemasons), but he wouldn't be able to provide any details on the group of people running around in gorilla suits or the hot go-go dancer with her boobs out.

HE LETS YOU BE THE CENTER OF ATTENTION

If a genius knocks over a Lego tower, can anyone hear it? Mr. Roboto is smart as hell, but drawing attention to it is not high on his agenda. He'd rather sit back and let you grab the spotlight. He's also twitchy and uncomfortable around new people. Your friends will later tell you they didn't realize when they first met him that they were meeting a genius. His one-liners blow everyone away. So do his random bursts of knowledge and fix-it. That kind of unassuming persona is really, really awesome.

HE GETS YOU INTELLECTUALLY

Think again if you're imagining two people sitting around debating Proust over soychinos. There are so many facets to intellect beyond all those other meaningless cultural badges that everyone lies about on their social networking profiles. The inside jokes are hilarious, multilayered, and easy. You go to see an art film, and Mr. Roboto says the exact pointed, snarky, uniquely tailored remark you were just about to say. Genius.

HE'S AN INVESTMENT RISK

You know those '80s makeover movies where the dorky friend helps make over the geek and then the geek leaves the girl for the popular girl but eventually ends up getting back together with her once he sees the error of his ways? Take out the happy ending, and this is a very real possibility. You start being his girlfriend, get him dressing better, acting better, socializing more normally at parties, and then . . . he all of a sudden gets pulled away by a cute girl who came to his roommate's band audition. Next time you'll make him sign a noncompete form.

HE CAN'T READ YOUR EMOTIONS

You cry. He checks his iPhone. You're nervous. He's as calm as a clam. You ask for a compliment. He explains to you why that's stupid. Mr. Roboto isn't wired to understand you. He knows Klingon and elvish and ancient Egyptian hieroglyphs, but when it comes to emotions, he's flat-out illiterate. Want empathy? Good luck. It's like teaching a snake how to touch-type; it's not in his nature.

HE ISN'T USED TO SHARING

Oh, sure, he'll loan you old back issues of *Mad* (he practically jizzed when he found out you liked them) and he'll supply you with days' worth of playlists, but he rarely shares a feeling. Even when he does, it's awkwardly rendered. It's not totally his fault; Mr. Roboto is as used to being as lone as the hermit he used to play in Dungeons & Dragons. You may find yourself reading books with titles like *The Emotionally Bankrupt Man* and *How to Talk When He Doesn't Want to Talk,* and rehearsing questions in front of the mirror. Incorporating a second party into his worldview is not going to happen unless you make it.

HOW TO END IT HARMONIOUSLY

WITH A COMPUTER

Mr. Roboto likes to be on the computer. If he can't find a computer, he'll use the nearest substitute, whether it's a cell phone, digital jukebox, slot machine, or Kodak Picture Maker! kiosk. For anyone else, this choice of medium might be considered cruel for a breakup. For Mr. Roboto, it's where he feels most comfortable. Send him a long e-mail missive and then be available for rapid-fire fallout via AIM and text. Make the offer to meet in person to follow up, though odds are he won't take you up on it. The next day he'll probably move on and come to think of it as no worse than a nasty comment thread.

WITH A PIE CHART

Mr. Roboto loves a clever presentation of information and would have a hard time choosing between a picture of a naked chick and a particularly clever Venn diagram. If you can present a logical reason for breaking up, backed by examples and measures of success, you're going to have a much easier time of it. If you can convince him that he's the one who came up with the brilliant theory, even better. We know it's dumb to play these kinds of games, and we do not mean to imply that Mr. Roboto is a witless rube. We're just saying to appeal to his rational side.

WITH AN IRRATIONAL FIT

Let's be honest: Mr. Roboto's stoicism can be really trying sometimes. We suppose that's why you're breaking up with him, but we just wanted to restate it one more time, in case you're sniffing his cardigan and getting all sobby. One day your patience will break. You will become the stuff of ex-girlfriend legend, the teacher who throws the fit in class that everyone remembers years later. You'll feel bad about this, but really. You're out of the relationship, and that's what you wanted. So he thinks you're a fluffernutter. So what?

HOW TO KEEP MAKING SWEET MUSIC TOGETHER

LET HIM FIGURE IT OUT

Mr. Roboto doesn't speak the same emotional language other folks do. It might be charming in a friend or acquaintance, but it's really grating in your day-to-day existence. Instead of going out of your way to correct him each time, which will only frustrate him because he'll feel nagged and frustrate you because you'll feel like a nag, try not reacting. At all. Take a deep breath and focus on something else. Whether by getting his ass kicked because he insists on wearing a shirt that says "God Is Dead" to a county fair or by "accidentally" being left off invites for other people's parties, he'll eventually get hip to social norms. Sometimes you can do the most good simply by being a silent example. In the meantime, be patient and try to be positive. You could think of him as an awkward albatross that needs help ordering pizza, or as an opportunity to see everything in a new and interesting way, like you do when having a friend visit from a foreign country.

LOSE YOUR IDEA OF TRADITIONAL ROMANCE

You're grown up enough not to expect daily poetry and teddy bears, yet still you'd like some emotional indication that you mean something to your partner. For anyone who's been involved with him for any period of time, we realize, that can be pretty hard to come by with Mr. Roboto. Here's the thing: He does really dig you; you're just not realizing it when he shows it. Every time he wrestles the phone out of your hands and insists that he can fix it himself when you try to call tech support, he is showing you that he wants to take care of you. We realize that not everyone can survive on that, so it's completely permissible to send him links with what you want for your birthday and ideas for sex positions. He may take three days doing elaborate research, but he'll get the job done.

RESPECT HIS LIMITS

Sometimes you wish each and every social relationship and even physical interaction didn't have to be so awkward, but Mr. Roboto *is* awkward. You wouldn't yell at your cat because it can't clean its own litter box. Work within Mr. Roboto's emotional schema rather than trying to fight it. Get to know when silence means "I'm freaking out!" and silence means "I'm comfortable and having a good time." We mention silence because most Mr. Robotos have as many different types of it as Eskimos have words for snow. Above all, remember that just because the way he communicates is different doesn't mean it's any less valid than yours.

FOR THE RECORD

aka Relationship Lessons from the School of Rock . . .

THERE ARE LOTS OF GOOD GUYS

Despite all those Fergie songs, there are still guys out there who are not players, have never been players, aren't players who say they're not players, and have no real agenda. Mr. Roboto may be weird at times and hard to relate to, but you've never doubted his motives, even when he was doing something shitty, like canceling a dinner so he could go into overtime on an online role-playing game.

IQ STANDARDS ARE A GOOD IDEA

Mr. Roboto is so brilliant that other men now seem dumb in comparison. Now that you know what good brains are like, it'll be hard to go back to dullards. Who will help you finish your crossword puzzles? Who will be reading good books and, by quiet example, encourage you to give up *Gossip Girl*, which you swear you're watching only to understand the tween demographic. It's going to be hard to fill those black socks and shoes.

KNOWING NERDS FOR FUN AND PROFIT

After dating Mr. Roboto, you will know the difference between fake nerd and real nerd and how much you can take of either. Maybe fake nerd is what you want. You'll take the style but not the hours spent following him around fossil and mineral shows, and for that we can't blame you. Maybe you want a partial nerd, who has some of the awkwardness but can control it with medication. There will be some very special few of you who want the whole nerd package. You, dear women, are probably related to the writer and illustrator of this book in some distant way. See you at Thanksgiving.

★★★ Reviews

What Critics Are Saying About Mr. Roboto

"He was so awkward. Sometimes I don't want to hang out with him if anyone else is there because it's an embarrassment to me that I am close to this person. If you want to talk about biomedical engineering—jackpot! Otherwise . . ."

—NADJA

"The thing about these guys is that one-on-one they're great; that's why people are attracted to them. When they're around other people it's like they have ADD and shut down."

—HOLLIE

"You do not bring them out into the real world."

—ERICA

YOUR MINI PRESS KIT

Mr. Roboto is the guy who . . .

✦ Wears what Urban Outfitters will co-opt in ten years.

✦ Has more health problems, real or imagined, than your average eighty-year-old.

✦ Chooses clothing based on utility rather than looks. A vest that can be turned into a router? He's got two.

✦ Is regarded with bemused suspicion by your mom and dad. They want to say "Dork!" but realize playground pejoratives are unbecoming in people their age.

✦ Backs up all your computer files instead of buying you flowers.

AFTER PARTY

How'd it go? Are your ears ringing? Is your voice hoarse? More important, did you get the drummer's phone number?

By now you've amassed more knowledge than Van Halen has lead singers. Will you use it for good or evil?

Whatever you do, and *whomever* you do, remember Rock 'n' Roll's Golden Rule:

> Be kind, be cool, and be sure to get documentation.

One day, when you're old and gray and happily coupled *or* a sexy senior citizen breaking hearts at the nursing home, you're going to want a little memento for the dashboard of your hoverpod. Make it a good one.

Yours in rock,
Erin and Heather

THANK YOU'S & ACKNOWLEDGMENTS

FROM THE AUTHOR

In no particular order, except words followed by spaces and then separated by semicolons and commas:

My sister Heather; my mom and dad; my best friend, Mary; the manufacturers, distributors, and sellers of Diet Coke and Trident Original Flavor; everyone at Nerve.com; my cats Creature and Drew; my friends in New York who will hopefully still like me enough to purchase this after having every social invitation rejected for well over a year; my friends on LiveJournal for their invaluable input; all the awesome ladies who shared their stories; family and friends too many to name but who are all the coolest; and last, Eric, for his endless patience, uncontested surrender of the living room, and unconditional support. I'll stop now before I break into power ballad, but please know that you are the best tour mate a girl could ever ask for.

FROM THE ILLUSTRATOR

My sister Erin; my mom and dad; my awesome friends who encouraged me throughout this project, especially Martina, Karell, Chassy, Charles, Marc, Stephen, Jenny, Jonathan, Andrew, Clara, Shek, and Nathan; the *Detroit Free Press* Sunday funny pages and *Mad* magazine for first introducing me to the art of parody; and last, the fine gentlemen of rock 'n' roll, may you never see these ridiculous caricatures of you.

FROM BOTH

We'd like to thank Brandi Bowles at Howard Morhaim; Gabrielle Moss, David Walker, and Meighan Cavanaugh at Tarcher/Penguin; and Katherine Obertance, for their hard work, encouragement, and all-around coolness, as well as all the hand-holding and neuroses-wrangling that comes with working with first-time authors.

ABOUT THE AUTHOR & ILLUSTRATOR

Though Will Smith was the DJ and Jazzy Jeff was the rapper, the roles weren't so clearly defined for this tome. It involved a lot of cross-collaboration and more than a few brainstorming sessions at Ace, Double Down, and other East Village dive institutions. If you see a funny caption or a particularly clever turn of phrase, be sure to compliment both sisters. Otherwise, one of us will get mad and rip down the other's INXS posters.

ABOUT THE AUTHOR

Erin Bradley is the author of "Miss Information," a weekly sex and dating advice column appearing on Nerve.com. When she's not at her day job in advertising (don't judge!) or writing freelance for various entertainment and tech publications, Erin can be found watching prison documentaries and *Golden Girls* reruns in her apartment in Manhattan's East Village. The first record she ever bought was a 45 rpm of "Eat It" by Weird Al. She lost her concert virginity during MC Hammer's "Please Hammer, Don't Hurt 'Em" tour, though she wishes it had happened during Aerosmith's 1975 cross-country "Toys in the Attic" road show featuring Foghat, Ted Nugent, REO Speedwagon, and Steppenwolf. Sadly, Ms. Bradley was still in utero at the time.

ABOUT THE ILLUSTRATOR

Heather Bradley is an award-winning designer and illustrator whose work has been published in print and online in *Seventeen*, *Teen*, and *Sex, Etc.*, and on iVillage.com. Her all-time favorite gig was at gURL.com, where she was the creative director and comic editor for over a thousand years in Internet time. When she's not drawing caricatures of aging rock stars, Heather teaches graphic design and illustration at the New York University School of Continuing and Professional Studies. She currently lives in Park Slope, Brooklyn, with her mineral/fossil collection and Monster, her cat. When she grows up, she wants to be Robert Smith of The Cure.

If you enjoyed this book, visit

www.tarcherbooks.com

and sign up for Tarcher's e-newsletter to receive special offers, giveaway promotions, and information on hot upcoming releases.

Great Lives Begin with Great Ideas

New at **www.tarcherbooks.com** and **www.penguin.com/tarchertalks**:

Tarcher Talks, an online video series featuring interviews with bestselling authors on everything from creativity and prosperity to 2012 and Freemasonry.

If you would like to place a bulk order of this book, call 1-800-847-5515.